MAKING TRACKS
THE RISE OF BLONDIE

BY

DEBBIE HARRY

CHRIS STEIN

AND

VICTOR BOCKRIS

A FRED JORDAN BOOK • A DELL TRADE PAPERBACK

Distributed by
Dell Publishing Co., Inc.
1 Dag Hammarskjold Plaza
New York, New York 10017

Dell ® TM 681510, Dell Publishing Co., Inc.
ISBN: 0-440-55150-1
Library of Congress Catalog Card No. 82-80116
Printed in the United States of America

Art Direction by Ken Deardoff

Design by Chris Stein and Victor Bockris.
All photographs taken, or in a few instances
set up, by Chris Stein.

First printing: May 1982
Second printing: June 1982

CONTENTS

ROOTS OF BLONDIE

I was Marilyn Monroe's Kid 7

Close Up At The Front: New York City 1965-1969 10

The Stillettoes 12

Becoming Blondie 19

Blondie on the Bowery 30

Getting Signed 43

The Iggy Tour 69

THE PLASTIC LETTERS PERIOD

First English Tour: May 17-June 3, 1977 77

Plastic Letters: May-October 1977 84

The World Tour: October 1977-February 1978 93

Australia 94

Thailand 106

Japan 112

Back to Europe 119

PARALLEL LINES

Parallel Lines 127

Heart of Glass European Tour 134

Back in the U. S. A. 138

Zipping Around Europe Again 144

From Eat To The Beat To Autoamerican 145

Eat To The Beat European Tour: 1979-1980 150

KOO KOO

New York City: January-August 1980 159

Autoamerican 161

Post Autoamerican: November 1980-August 1981 166

The Ghost of Sunday Man 178

New York 178

Debbie at home.

ROOTS OF BLONDIE

I WAS MARILYN MONROE'S KID

I don't know exactly where I came from because I don't know who my natural parents are. Chris thinks I'm definitely an alien because I fit the description in a book he read of a race of females who were put on this planet from space. I was adopted when I was three months old through an agency (my first agent) in Miami, Florida, by Catherine and Richard Harry, transferred to another agency in New Jersey where they picked me up. My first memory is of the hotel we went to on vacation where they had small farm animals like ducks, chickens, and goats, which in my memory were enormous elephants and such, in pens. I was apparently a very beautiful baby. The doctor told my parents to watch out for my bedroom eyes—"I can just feel it," he said, "she has something." They had a good laugh over that.

When I was three or four years old Mom and Dad told me I was adopted, but it didn't bother me at the time, although that is when I had my first memorable psychic experience. We lived in Hawthorne, New Jersey, where I spent almost every day in the yard digging in my sand pile, daydreaming, and swinging. One day I started hearing voices coming from a brick fireplace my dad had built, telling me complex mathematical information. I ran into the house to tell my mother what I'd heard and how important it was. She laughed as I tried to verbalize what I thought I had heard because it sounded ridiculous. The exhilarating physical sensation this psychic contact had given me was gone and I was left feeling oddly empty. Earth to Deb . . .

I always knew I was a singer. When I began singing with the radio I was struck by the fact that I knew the next note before it was played. Lying in bed tuned in to the "Hit Parade," I started to play the sing-the-note-before-it's-played game to test myself—listening to my black plastic Emerson radio which was emblazoned with a gold G clef on its face. After I turned six I became an ugly little thing, putting on some chubs, wearing corrective shoes, and being a tomboy as I recall. But I'm glad I was a playful kid more interested in my bike than looking pretty.

There I was, a fat cherubic soprano getting it on with the Christian Soldiers in the church choir. I loved singing so much I won the choir's perfect attendance award, a silver cross, truly earned by my parents for getting me to practice every week. Around this time my sister was born.

When I was eleven we moved to another neighborhood in Hawthorne which put me in a different school district. The new girls were much more sophisticated. They wore bras and full skirts with crinolines. I had never even considered wearing a bra, garter belt, or stockings, but it was this introduction to underwear that made me become aware of outerwear. Suddenly stockings and bras had a place in my drawers, and as soon as I started buying my own clothes in seventh grade, everything had to be black—except the hair. You can easily imagine the feud between mother and me at this fashionable choice. We always had especially heated debates about clothes.

One afternoon while we sat in the kitchen drinking coffee my Aunt Helen said I looked like a movie star, which thrilled me and fueled another secret fantasy about Marilyn Monroe possibly being my natural mother. I always thought I was Marilyn Monroe's kid. I felt physically related and akin to her long before I knew she had been adopted herself. Of course my continual participation in this maternal fantasy has changed drastically as I've grown up and discovered that quite a few adopted girls have the same notion. But why Marilyn and not Lana Turner, Carole Lombard, Jayne Mansfield? Maybe it was Marilyn's need for immense doses of demonstrative love that is the common denominator between us. Although that doesn't fit me because I got loads of love. My parents had to put up with some stupid shit from me like I've always had this sense of destiny, and when I felt I wasn't being appreciated I'd tell them, "You'll be sorry you talked to me like this when I'm rich and famous." They would laugh. At least I kept them entertained.

I feared and hated school passionately. The boring and important monster, like carrying a weight on your back fed by sick teachers for twelve years. False pressures keep the kids within margins simulating relevance to the funky bumpy world. School was like treading water to me. Art classes were my favorites, but painting/drawing wasn't considered important. Having shaken off the fat years I made baton twirler and was voted the prettiest girl in my senior class. Apart from that I didn't have very much going for me in high school. I felt everybody was trying to limit what I was before I tried anything.

My hair became the outward sign of my flamboyant nature. There was no color I didn't try, including green, even if that was a mistake. The first bleaching was in 1959, with a peroxide-ammonia cocktail resulting in a sunny orange color, and I never looked back, although the chemical blend became the professional version. When as a freshman I started to draw attention to myself, with the orange hair and mostly black clothes, I thought I was on my way. And when Sonny and Cher came out with those hairy vests I definitely knew I had something going, because I had designed and made one just like theirs a year before.

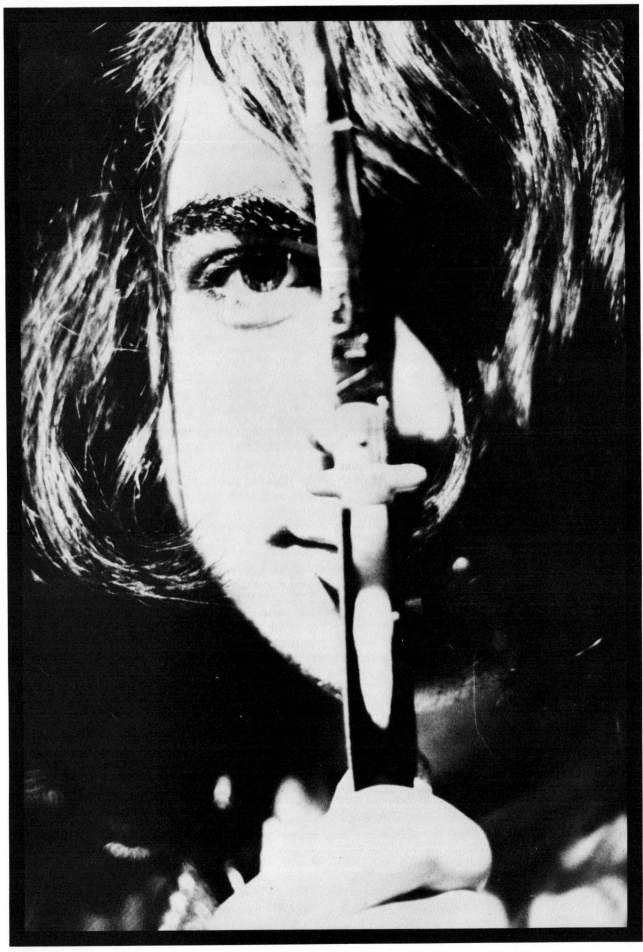

Chris at home.

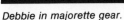
Debbie in majorette gear.

I always dressed intuitively and emotionally, but sometimes with disastrous results. Looks change just like fashion, and at that time I did not fit into the mainstream image. An oval face was considered beautiful, not a broad round blob like mine, which earned me the nickname Moon. Exotic makeup experimental in my hands caused my closest girlfriends to refuse to be seen with me. I guess all those penciled beauty marks were beyond . . . I must have looked like a connect-the-dots drawing in 3-D.

As a teenager the one thing that I loved was listening to rock'nroll. I wasn't old enough to go to concerts but that wasn't so bad if you could go to dances, and 1959–1965 was a great time to be a rock'nroll teenager. Except for Murray the K's shows at the Brooklyn Fox, concerts weren't such a big thing. Radio was at its peak. Every show was in heavy competition to discover the newest, wildest sound on plastic. Payola was a public joke, music was mono. The first rock stuff I got into was Frankie Lyman Doo Wop during the fifties. Later my dancing friends and I did the Strand, the Hully Gully, the Swim, the Jump, the Bop, the Watusi and the Twist—kicked off by the Mashed Potatoe, which, when seen for the first time, caused some kind of scandal at school: "You're dancing like a nigger girl," they said. "You can't do that!" Until that time expressing how the music made you feel solo hadn't been done. No one had ever moved on the dance floor without a partner.

Chris grew up on Winky Dink, Howdy Doody, and Abbott and Costello in Brooklyn. His mother was a beatnik painter and window designer. His father was a salesman and frustrated artist. It was a typical liberal artistic household. They weren't at all religious.

Chris wanted to be an Egyptologist. He was bored and sat in his room playing most of the time. His parents gave him his first guitar when he was eleven. He taught himself to play and got turned on to folk music and civil-rights campaigns. When he was fifteen his father died of a heart attack. He was only in his fifties, but he was a very sensitive man and his inability to release his creativity had put a great strain on him.

Chris may have been bored as a kid but he was always in bands making music. He used to go out into the streets and pull speakers out of discarded TVs and hook them up to one beat-up old record player in his room. The whole room, which was painted black, was covered with speakers. He used to blast them as loud as he could; naturally the neighbors got upset. Chris could smoke pot and have all his friends over. It got so bad everybody thought his mother was running a den of iniquity for all these children having jam sessions in her basement, and she became the neighborhood bad person. One day when Chris'd just finished playing "Sunshine Superman" ten times in a row, the next-door neighbor had a nervous breakdown, came running over, and started smashing their door in with a hammer screaming, "AAAAAHHHHHHHH!" Someone from his family had to come and drag him away.

Chris hated school more than I did. He acted out all his most rebellious impulses, wore steel-rimmed glasses, and told the teachers it was just too bad he hadn't done his homework. He was the first kid to get thrown out of his school for having really long hair. His mother was never uptight about this. At the time, there was a big test case in which some kid was suing his school for being thrown out for having long

Chris with guitar.

hair. Chris's principal got very paranoid, and the school called him up, told him he could come back, wouldn't have to take gym, etc. He was happy to be out, so he didn't go back to public school. We both think childhood is murder. As soon as most kids begin to develop any unique signs of personality, they get targeted for abuse and oppression more than anyone else in society. They're helpless, usually walked-over toys.

CLOSE UP AT THE FRONT: NEW YORK CITY 1965-1969

As soon as I graduated high school my parents sent me to a two-year college. After graduation my main ambition was to move straight to New York and begin to try being an artist. After my first couple of straight jobs, one with a Gift Mart and then with the BBC, I worked in a downtown head shop. Since it was the only head shop in the world, everyone came in. In fact, Chris had been there the day before it opened. He was riding the subway in from Brooklyn to hang out in Greenwich Village, going through his *December's Children* period, playing along with

Beatles and Stones records in between standing in cold gray doorways armed with a Harmony Hollow-Body f-Hole guitar and a Silvertone amp. During those years he learned from a cross section of guitarists from John Fahey and Lester Flatt to the Lovin' Spoonfuls and Bob Dylan. He was going to a private school called Quintano's, but he was still a goof-off.

During the sixties, I saw and heard a lot of music that left indelible impressions on me, like The Doors when they stood on a birthday cake-like riser at the Filmore and played every song perfectly while the audience watched spellbound; Lou Reed at the Electric Circus when he played for hours with the original Velvet Underground and Nico, backed by Andy Warhol's Lightshow, and you couldn't help feeling a different sense of time because they created an overpowering fresh environment. I'll never forget seeing Janis Joplin with Big Brother and the Holding Company at the Anderson Theater in 1967, when she grabbed a bottle of Southern Comfort off the top of the upright piano, took a belt, and went straight into "Ball and Chain" begging "Take my heart!" Chris saw Janis at the Filmore. We also both saw Jimi Hendrix, who I think is definitely the best electric guitar player. His material stands up in every way today. I was painting then, but beginning to feel music more, so I started painting sound. But sound had to be painted on walls, not canvas, so I decided to move into music, stopped painting, and spent more time in clubs with live music.

Sometimes I used to buy *Backstage,* which listed open calls for Broadway shows like the one for *Hair* when thousands of kids showed up and stood on an endless line. I didn't know about agents, and I went to a few of these auditions on full-sized stages in Broadway theaters, but I never got further than singing "Oh, la-da-da," before a voice would boom "Thank you very much," out of the dark, and I would trot off, having waited in line a whole day being sweaty and nervous, along with all these show-biz hopefuls. Looking back that scene makes me think of a convention of bag women.

In 1966 I joined a group with a floating membership called The Tri-Angels, which was held together under the leadership of Charlie Nothing on Sopranino Sax. In 1967 Paul Klien put together a folk rock group called Wind in the Willows. One night we were cruising around and I started singing harmony with the music and became a member of the group. Meanwhile, before spending the summer of love in San Francisco, Chris had been playing briefly in the Morticians, who went on to become The Left Banke.

From 1968–69 I worked as a waitress in Max's Kansas City. That was another good place to see and hear everything. I served The Jefferson Airplane their dinner the night before they went to Woodstock. The next day, as I headed up to the Festival, Chris was having his physical examination at the draft board. By this time, he'd taken a lot of acid and was experiencing long periods of seeing everything as cosmic dust, so he'd received his draft notice in an insane asylum, where he spent three months after flipping out completely at the beginning of '69 when he was twenty. This was mostly a delayed reaction to his father's death. He was also very paranoid about being drafted, but he didn't really have anything to worry about, because at the psychiatric interview he was able to insist that he had everything on their list. Anyway, he got out of there with a 4F and rushed up to Woodstock, although we still didn't bump into each other.

When I worked at Max's I loved all the people from Andy Warhol's Factory, like Eric Emerson, Viva, Ingrid, Taylor Mead, Ultra Violet, International Velvet, Candy Darling, and all the superstars. I was just a baby growing up in the middle of this whole incredible scene, watching Andy Warhol's eight-hour movies and listening to all kinds of fantastic music very close up at the front. I looked semi-exotic enough for an interesting evening, but I still didn't know who I was and I often couldn't talk.

Wind in the Willows recorded two albums, the first of which was released by Capitol Records. At least I was in the music business, which is where I wanted to be, but I wanted to do hotter stuff than the Willows, so after a year plus with them I went my own way. Sometimes I would stand up a bit tipsy at some strange bar (never where I was known) and sing along with the piano player or band, but they'd always throw me out eventually. Somehow, I knew I couldn't do it right yet, being depressed and upset most of the time I could hardly open my mouth with-

out bursting into tears—like singing the blues, but this was ridiculous.

During the sixties I was still unsure of exactly who I was, which made it difficult to deal with other people and kept me out of whack in relation to myself as well. This was debilitating and painful. In *Popism,* his history of the sixties, Andy Warhol says Emile de Antonio encouraged him before he was discovered. Emile was the first person to give me encouragement too. He's a remarkable, wonderful maniac. We talked about my problems and I said I thought it would take me two years to work them all out. Emile replied that it would take more like eight. I was horrified by his thinking that I was such a nurd and got pissed as hell, but he was right.

While tottering around Max's with my trays of lamb chops, and, after that, working as a Playboy Bunny for nine months, I fooled around with drugs and was consequently often half asleep, but at least I wasn't so tense and nervous the whole time. Getting high relieved this constant strain, enabling me to leave my apartment and hold down a regular job. During this period I began to outwit and outgrow whatever was confusing me. However, after a while, paying for the drugs and doing them became a bigger drag than the problems I was trying to solve. I was using drugs in my life, but I didn't want them to become my life. A lot of people don't make this distinction and the drugs do become their life. I got smart and stopped. I guess I had to go the limit before my instincts could reactivate.

By 1969 something had come to a dead end. It seemed like I had reached the entrance to a tunnel, and I could either go down into the tunnel and continue, or I could take this little winding road off to the side. It was important for me to be an artist, and I was singing at a time when Janis Joplin was out there and she died; I kept thinking about Janis and Billie Holiday and the blues. All that sadness and tragedy just kept going through my head. I love the blues, but I didn't want to sing them. I wanted to entertain people, have a good time, and be happy. Those singers were forced to live out the reality of their blues.

So what else does a girl do at the end of the sixties? I wanted music that popped and as a Bunny I was losing my hop. I just wanted out. I moved to a $75-a-month studio apartment, but eventually the real estate broker who handled the building came around and said I could stay there for no rent whatsoever if I made it with him on a regular basis. I thought, Oh shit! I'm not going to get involved with this. So, burned-out but determined to regain my strength, I packed everything and moved upstate to live outside Woodstock in Phoenicia with my pregnant girlfriend.

The same thing happened to a lot of people at the end of the sixties. Nothing was happening, so there was nothing to do. Everything was fucked up with Nixon and the end of the war. It was a tremendously down period and we all had to shake off the freakouts that occurred in '68 and '69. I took a sabbatical from the whole scene for three years, during which time Chris, having been released from the nuthouse, went on welfare and, sponsored by the division of vocational rehabilitation, was studying photography at the School of Visual Arts, and making some of the connections that would eventually lead to our meeting.

THE STILLETTOES

It took me some time to readjust. I got the old blow-ups and put on a lot of weight. By the time I left Phoenicia in 1970 you couldn't tell the difference between me and my pregnant girlfriend. I moved back in with my parents for a year. They were both working so I was the housekeeper. It felt good to be home again. I was twenty-five and taking stock of my situation. I still knew I wanted to sing, but wasn't quite able to release my voice.

In 1971 I helped my parents move to upstate New York, then rented a room for myself from a truck driver, underneath the George Washington Bridge on the Jersey side of the river in Fort Lee. While living there I worked in a health spa. Shortly after this I met a young car salesman who arranged for me to move into my own apartment. I started going out with him and soon, although I kept my apartment, I was virtually living with him. Suddenly I was all set in a new life again with my job and boyfriend.

The job was a bust but that wasn't all. We discovered we weren't meant for each other, and I moved back into my own apartment. I went to cosmetician school, and started a job in a friend's beauty salon in Jersey. My ex kept calling me in the middle of the night—possessiveness was a major reason we broke up—to make sure I was home alone. It's a good thing I was working in a salon because I wasn't getting any beauty sleep.

In 1972 I started coming back into New York to visit friends. It was the same scene, but with different faces. The New York Dolls were ruling the roost at the Mercer Arts Center. One day at Max's, I heard from Janis that Elda Gentile, Holly Woodlawn, and Diane, who was living with the Dolls' vocalist David Johansen, had a girl trio called Pure Garbage, so next time I ran into Elda at a show at Max's I asked her if I could come and see them. She said okay, and we exchanged phone numbers. She never called, so I finally called her up and said, "What's happening with your group? I'd love to come and see it." She said, "We broke up." I said, "Oh, well, if you ever want to do anything let me know, because I might like to do something." She said, "Okay, I don't know." She never called me. I called her back and she said, "Yeah, why don't you come over and we'll get together with this other girl I know, Roseanne, and try to do something." That's how I got back into the music business. I had nothing left to lose and everything to gain. Singing has always been an obsession with me. I would wake up every morning with one thought haunting me, knowing that if I didn't try I would never forgive myself. I knew I had a voice but it was somewhere south of my chin at the time. Only singing could give life to that mood, that minute that

was me. I knew that trying to satisfy this obsession was the only thing I could do to make me feel right.

While I was still living in New Jersey, Elda, Rosie Ross, and I formed the original Stillettoes. We didn't get the name right away. Elda came up with it later. We tried to be a dance band. The original group included Tommy and Jimmy from The Miamis, Timothy Jackson, a drummer who also manufactured dresses, and Youngblood. Tony Ingrassia, a director who had a number of underground successes off-Broadway, was our choreographer. He worked on us to project mood and gave us a cohesive look, so that by the time we started gigging together we each had a stage concept. Elda wanted to make us a campy, kitsch materialization of the *True Confessions* heart-throb garbage girl who's fucked and abandoned, widowed or unmarried; Rosie was into rhythm and blues soul music; I wanted a combination of the aggressive Shangri-Las' rock and the round solid vocals of an R&B girl group. The overall idea was to be entertaining and danceable. Rock dancing was nonexistent. Disco was just starting to get a real hold on people.

Meanwhile Chris saw a poster, in the lobby of the School of Visual Arts, for a New York Dolls show at the Mercer Arts Center and went to the show. Eric Emerson and The Magic Tramps opened the set and Chris liked the flamboyant nature of their act. In his opinion the Dolls primarily appealed to girls. So Chris got Eric a gig at the Visual Arts Center's Christmas party, became friends with him, met Jane Forth, and fell in with the people who hung out on the periphery of the Dolls. Then he became Eric's roadie, and that's how Chris broke his teeth.

One night The Magic Tramps left Mercer Arts to play a lesbian bar in Passaic. Eric and some of the band were in a small car, Chris was in a panel truck with all the equipment. As they were driving everyone got more and more screwed up until Eric started playing chicken with them. They were going about forty miles an hour past lampposts, then at lampposts, and finally into a lamppost. Like the proverbial drunk who falls off a horse-drawn cart, they were all so fucked up they went with the flow, and Chris luckily only broke his teeth instead of destroying his face. Nobody got killed, but they were out in the sticks and the lamppost was embedded halfway through the van, so the police took them to the hospital. The bass player, Wayne, had a cut, but he was so covered with glitter his green beard hid it. They finally located the cut, sewed it up and sent him out, but he also had amnesia. Five hours later, bloody and dazed, The Magic Tramps played the lesbian gig, but none of them knew what was going on.

Chris was invited to the second Stillettoes gig at the Boburn Tavern on W. 28th Street by Elda, who was the mother of Eric's children. The most striking thing about collaboration is that it often happens in dreams. A microsecond of dream will unfold an elaborate scene in a flash. That can also happen in daytime when the immediacy of a situation connects a whole chain of events. It's an amazing form of communication and it happened between Chris and me the first time we saw each other when I was singing and he was in the audience at the Boburn. I couldn't

Stillettoes artifact: Knife as heel.

see his face, only the outline of his head, but I could feel him looking at me and I was very nervous so I delivered a lot of songs to him. We had a psychic connection right away, which struck me particularly because I'd previously only had such strong psychic connections with girlfriends.

It was Elda's idea to ask Chris to join the group. I hadn't spoken to him after the gig that night because he'd been with another girl, and not having seen his face I wasn't even sure if it was the same guy. A couple of days later she called him. Chris was semi-playing with The Magic Tramps, but he wasn't committed to them so he agreed to play full time with us, partly because he liked me, but I didn't know that at the time.

He was living in a $125-a-month apartment for welfare recipients on the Lower East Side and letting Eric stay there with him. Chris and Eric were the only freaks in the building which was full of lower-income families. Everybody thought they were horrible and was terrified the freaks were going to rape their daughters. Eric didn't help relations with the neighbors by rushing out and screaming in the halls at 4 A.M., or coming around to the back of the building in the middle of the night and yelling, "Throw down my drugs! They're in the drawer!" "I can't find them," Chris would yell back, and lights would snap on all over the building as they carried on this fren-

zied exchange: "No. No. Over *there.*" Things got progressively worse. The neighbors hated them, the super was freaking, and Eric *was* a maniac, although Chris loved living with him because he brought constant excitement into the apartment. He was always importing teenage girls, feeding them quaaludes, and fucking them. Or bringing home a girl with her boyfriend and fucking the girl in the loft bed while the boyfriend would sit there stupefied.

After a while I moved back to New York, renting an apartment on Thompson Street that Rosie had found. Chris helped me move my three gray cats and furniture over from New Jersey. The cats represented the trinity of the heart, the soul, and the conscience. Gray Girl, who was always paranoid, was the conscience. Daniel, the leader, was the heart, and the fat, human third one, Sunday Man, was the soul of the group. Chris and I hadn't become lovers yet, but through working together we'd become friends. He knew I was nervous that my past would catch up with me. The all-night phone calls continued, so he said I could stay at his apartment if I would feel safer. However, after a while the Jersey car salesman came to his senses. I think he felt bad about what he'd done and didn't want any more hassles, so after I moved to Thompson Street I never saw him again.

I've always felt the environment one lives in has an effect on what one does, and this certainly was proved true in the initial stages of my collaboration with Chris. While I lived on Thompson Street he had that apartment at the beginning of First Avenue. The walk we took along Houston Street between the two apartments gave spontaneous birth to the first songs we wrote together. I was walking to his house one day when I started working up a song called "Platinum Blonde." By the time I got there I had the lyrics and melody so we started fooling around with it right away. Movement, like walking, driving, or listening to the bump, spin, hiss of the laundromat or motors, has always been an inspiration for lyrics. On his way over to Thompson Street Chris passed a fence on Houston where a demented writer used to leave rambling notes to the Department of Social Security concerning the troubles of his niece. Each note was dated and Chris collected them daily for a year, until he had a whole bag of notes in which the writer carefully repeated the same numbers. Watching his mind decompose was a fascinating art piece, and, though we didn't use any of his lines in songs, they were definitely another inspiration.

The Stillettoes period was general chaos. We attracted the most fucked up and interesting people and had the cruddiest equipment. Apart from the names I've already mentioned, there was Tom, a straight hippie who loaned Chris a really beautiful deco Supro-Ozark guitar, but after he had a sex change and became Vanessa he decided he wanted it back. I remember one day getting dragged all over the Lower East Side for this photo session and ending up sitting on piles of tires in an empty lot. That's a pretty appropriate picture.

By now Eric had met Barbara Winter—ex of Edgar —and had moved out of Chris's apartment to a loft up the street from Max's. He had originally run into her at a party but she was with another man and had given Eric her card. A few weeks later he went to the Dolls' Halloween party at the Waldorf Astoria dressed like an angel, with gold wings over a gold lamé stretch outfit, wearing gold jewelry and gold glitter on his face and carrying a gold guitar. He got up onstage and was singing along but he was so happy he kept on for too long and the promoter came on to drag him off. Eric hit him over the head with his guitar. Everyone in the audience went "Yaaaaay!" Then Eric charged off in a blue Mustang belonging to the girl he was with and started barreling through the Lincoln Tunnel. I think he was actually bouncing off the walls as he went through. Anyway, the cops picked him up on the other side and were making him walk the straight line in his angel's outfit, so he called Barbara Winter and asked her to come bail him out. After that, they started hanging around together. She helped support him and was very nice. They lived in that loft for a couple of years. One time Eric was stoned out of his mind, lying naked and getting screwed in front of a picture window on the second floor overlooking Park Avenue South. It was during lunch hour, and hundreds of business people on their lunch breaks gathered to watch. Traffic was backed up for blocks and the police were hammering on the door. Eric also used to rehearse there, but his space was right up against the wall of an apartment building so, try as they did to soundproof the walls, they could never make the neighbors happy enough.

After Tony Ingrassia stopped directing The Stillettoes, Roseanne got fed up and quit. We kept changing musicians, which was very frustrating, so the group broke up for a while. Roseanne and I tried to go on working and looked for another girl. We also went to some auditions. Once we somehow went to an audition for Bette Midler in a midtown mirrored dance studio. A choreographer started teaching us a little dance step. I said, "Roseanne, we're singers, this is an audition for dancers." But she just shrugged. We sort of caught on to the tap dance routine, but neither of us were tap dancers and this was a high-caliber audition. One of the girls had flown in from L.A. just for the chance to audition for Bette. There were about thirty professionally trained dancers and singers who wanted to be on Broadway, tapping along next to me and Roseanne, who believed in rock'nroll forever. We were The Stillettoes! Why were we learning this tap dance? We must've looked hysterical because we never got to sing a fucking note. Before we got through the tap routine a voice just said, "Er . . . thank you very much," and that was it. The funny thing was, at the end of the audition, Bette came in. She was all smiles, friendly and sparkling, and shook hands with each girl who'd tried out. When she got to me and Roseanne she said, "Oh, I've heard about you, and I wish you a lot of luck." Since I'd only just heard of us myself, I was very surprised.

By this time Chris was living with me on Thompson Street. I liked living with him because he wasn't overly possessive. He didn't have an extreme macho attitude, and we had fun together. We laughed at the same things, yet we had differences of opinion and respect for each other. Many people become so intent on achieving they lose all perspective. Our connection marked a turning point for both of us, but when I first met him I wasn't interested in a deep love relationship, having had a horrible affair. I was determined to be independent. There was no pressure.

Chris and I balance each other. His logic never fails to put things in perspective for me. He's able to see that if you stay at one thing long enough you automatically get a chance. I'd never stayed at one thing for more than a year. He's also a much more laid-back person. In turn I'm able to deal with the kinds of things that he worries about. So we help each other. He's sane where I'm crazy and I'm sane where he's crazy.

I can't believe that our relationship not only survived but incredibly it's improved since the first year we lived together. Sometimes we would have huge fights, staggering angrily around the room swinging and screaming at each other, but basically Chris remained calmer than I did. He would tell me that I was wrong to try to knock him down. For some reason I listened to him and it worked out.

Around this time the Mercer Arts Center collapsed. The center was integrally linked to the Broadway Central hotel, which had had a glorious history but had now become a crumbling structure occupied by

Eric Emerson.

Eric's arm: Stillettoes is written in magic marker between the two halves of his dagger tattoo.

15

Stillettoes on the street: Amanda, Elda, Debbie, 1974.

The Magic Tramps. Left to right, Sesu, Wayne, Eric, Larry, Kevin.

CBGBs bathroom.

Stillettoes at CBGBs.

welfare recipients. It was so old and decrepit from years of people pissing on the floor and throwing up in the corner that it just caved in. Supposedly Larry and Sesu from The Magic Tramps were inside Mercer rehearsing when it actually fell down; clutching their instruments as plaster crashed around their heads like a scene from an earthquake movie, they barely escaped.

Nothing came of our collaboration with Roseanne. Then one day Elda was having auditions to get The Stillettoes back together. So Chris and I went by Eric's place to check it out. We made friends with Elda again. She had found a third girl, Amanda Jones, whom everybody liked, so we started working with her. Amanda was great-looking. The whole act became more gaudy and tacky and the press started coming around. By that time we had Fred Smith on bass. Elda had called up an ad he'd placed and everybody liked Fred. Billy O'Connor was on drums. We had known him from the Boburn in the very early days.

When we started playing CBGB's it was a biker bar. Nobody went there but bikers. There were only a few bands that needed a place to play so they played there. The stage was then off to the side and much closer to the bar. There was a pool table in the back where the stage is now, and the bathrooms were parallel to the pool table. The stage was small and tiered on three levels, putting the drummer up in the rafters on a tiny platform, beneath which was another platform for the guitars, etc, and a third eight inches above the floor for the singer, or whatever.

I remember everybody's reaction to seeing Television for the first time. Elda said, "Oh, they dress like old men. They wear baggy pants!" These guys dressed like Bowery bums while everybody else was semi-glitter wearing tight pants or pantyhose. Average dress for a guy in those days was five pairs of pantyhose and no pants, and these guys came out in these shitty rags. They all wore ripped-up old shirts, except Richard Hell who would wear a ripped-up James Brown frilled satin shirt, and they all had short hair. As far as expertise went they were the same as the other bands, although they had a slightly different sound that was very droney. They weren't trying to be slick.

Meanwhile Eric and Barbara moved out of their loft on Park Avenue South to a hi-rise terrace apartment down on the Lower West Side by the river. When they moved out Eric ran around the loft singlehandedly destroying all the work he had done on it. He punched holes in the walls with his bare fists and smashed everything up.

All the way through The Stillettoes I had a '67 Camaro I'd inherited from my mother. We didn't have enough to keep it up properly so it gradually

Winter on the Lower East Side.

deteriorated. Having the car was a great luxury and it saved our sensibilities. We used to take pleasant little day trips to Coney Island or other beaches. For a long time, while I lived on Thompson Street, I used to park down on Washington Street in Tribeca, near Eric's new apartment. Parking was almost another full-time job on three mornings a week, getting up at six-thirty to make the move by seven before the car got towed: once those hooks and chains are on your car they stay on until the car reaches Pier #76—the Tombs for vagrant cars.

Getting up and moving the car in the early morning had its advantages. I used to sit there for three hours every other day of the week, waiting for the alternate side of the street parking regulations to take effect. To get a place that was good for two of three days, I'd sit in the car until the street cleaner came, then swerve out of the way, and repark as soon as he passed. That way, I'd get a parking place good for two days and no ticket. Most of my songs were written while I waited in the early morning (engine on in the winter) for the sweeper. This is a poem I wrote about one of Eric Emerson's girlfriends, Jane Forth, while sitting in the car:

I've seen you in the morning
walking your boy to school
I'm sitting in my Chevy, wondering what to do
We know we've seen each other

yet we never speak
Your boy goes in the door
with your kiss on his cheek.
Early morning memories are not what I awake
But old, decrepit ideals
which I can't seem to shake.

After oversleeping one morning I got to my car just as the tow truck guy was stepping down out of his truck with chains in hand. I started to run, screaming "No! No! Don't take it. I'm here!" He could see I was about to have a major breakdown, so he said, "Okay . . . okay . . . I'll let you go this time, but don't let it happen again." He turned toward the next suspect vehicle and stalked away, rattling his chains like a ghost. The sound made goose bumps on my arms and sent chills up my spine. But see, he didn't have them *on* the car yet. Because once the tow man bends over and snaps his rig on your car, that's it. You can threaten suicide. It doesn't make any difference. Your car is in chains.

The Stillettoes finally broke up over the usual business and personality clashes. Elda was working with a manager, leaving Amanda and me out of the picture, so we decided to leave the group. I went and told Elda. After that I finally gave up on the sixties girl-group idea, because it can't be done again. The people who did it best were the black chicks anyway.

Stillettoes. Left to right, Amanda, Billy, Elda, Chris, Fred, Debbie.

18

Debbie and Chris.

I finally had to face the fact that I'm not black. It wasn't easy.

The Dolls were playing around. We went to their 1973–74 New Year's show at the Academy of Music. They were introduced by Shoo Bee Doo, a four-year-old baby in a diaper. He represented the New Year. Shoo Bee Doo was a great little kid who hung out with the Dolls and was in some photos with them. Unfortunately one day Shoo Bee Doo was alone in the apartment and the heat got turned off. He was cold, went to light the stove, and blew himself up. The word was soon out on the street; everybody was very sad about it.

BECOMING BLONDIE

When Chris and I left The Stillettoes in the summer of 1974, the rest of the band (Billy O'Connor on drums and Fred Smith on bass) helped Elda get a few things together auditioning people, then came with us. We were moving on, but we still had no specific idea what we were doing. We just kept playing with different musicians. Everyone was still so bored at the time we never thought about making it. Who cared? We just kept playing around sporadically.

Ivan Krall (later in Patti Smith) joined to fill out the sound, but he only lasted three months. Around this time our drummer, Billy, had grave doubts about his choice of career and he started to flake out. It was sort of like roulette—your turn to go crazy.

After Eric left Chris's apartment, the place had cooled out for about twenty minutes; then we ran into Tommy Erdelyi, whom we knew from Mercer Arts Center when his name was Scotty and he was in a band called Butch. Tommy now worked in Performance Studios right around the corner from Max's on East 20th and he invited us to rehearse there. He said he thought I had a great voice for rock'nroll and also that he had a band in Queens called The Ramones. They'd taped some stuff at Performance with Tommy engineering but they didn't know where to play in the city. At that point we were the second band after Television to play CBGB's under its New Wave policy, thanks to Television's bass player, Richard Hell, who'd been going out with Elda and had told us about the place. We invited Tommy and his group to play with us at CBGB's. From then on we often played there together. The Ramones were always well organized with a professional approach to their gigs.

Chris sublet his First Avenue apartment to Tommy. He was quiet, but when more Ramones moved in things went bananas again very fast. There were

19

David Johanson and Gorilla Rose in front of CBGBs.

Debbie in the subway.

Bulletin Board in the Thompson Street apartment.

screams, holes punched in the wall and windows broken. Reports reached us that a chick locked a guy out in his underwear and he pissed in the hall, so it was like having Eric back.

One night Eric, Chris, and Barbara went to see The Dictators at Popeye's Spinach Factory in Brooklyn. Eric got raging drunk, jumped up onstage with The Dogs, and tore his shirt off. Then The Dictators came onstage and their big fat roadie jumped on too and sang "Wild Thing." That was Dick Manitoba. Everybody in the room was completely drunk. It was like a fraternity party. After that Manitoba sang with The Dictators. Meanwhile Eric was getting progressively crazier. He would go out in an expensive suit but get so frenzied he would rip it to shreds. He also developed a tendency to bite everybody.

Nineteen seventy-four was the non-period of punk. Television, The Ramones, and us, either as Angel and the Snake (for two gigs) or with no name, were just playing around. Then we did two or three gigs with a couple of girls, Julie and Jackie, and we all had blond hair so that's when we started fooling around with the name Blondie. I had always been called "blondie" by assorted motorists and truck drivers and thought it was a good name, a natural (HA!), so easy to remember. We played at a club uptown, Brandy's 11, with Tish and Snookie Bellomo, who later went on to open Manic Panic and star in the Sic Fuks. That's

when we were Blondie and the Banzai Babies. Tish and Snookie sang backup with us, on and off for over a year and a half. They drifted in and out of a lot of bands and still do. Our hottest number was "Lady Marmalade." We were a dance band, but to tell the truth we were so bad that to call us a garage band, to call us a band, was a great compliment. We were a gutter band—a sewer band's a closer description. We weren't getting any reviews, didn't have any support from any record company, didn't know anybody in the business, Chris's guitar cost $40, he didn't even have an amplifier, and our drummer couldn't make up his mind whether he wanted to be a drummer or a doctor.

Eventually he decided to be a doctor, so we put an ad in the *Voice* for a new drummer and auditioned the fifty applicants. Most of the guys who came in were schrumpy-looking schlumps in fringe jackets without the fringe. We had to throw some of them out of the room. Clem Burke was the last arrival. He was eighteen. We liked him immediately because he was one of the very best players, but more importantly he had a charismatic quality. He was also the only one who had on fancy shoes. Clem was definitely what we were looking for. His father was a drummer in a society band and he was a show biz drummer. Keith Moon, the biggest influence on his playing style and outlook, fit right in with the rock greats

Debbie as Punkmate of the Month.

Chris and I emulated. As someone who used to go to Woolworth's to buy bin albums by The Shangri-Las and The Ventures, he fell in enthusiastically with our plans to form a pop group that aimed to modernize AM radio sounds. Clem never wanted anything else but to be a pop star.

We shared a small rehearsal space in a garment center building on West 37th street with a band made up of rich kids who had all this great new equipment and did gigs on Fire Island and at colleges, etc. One day we came in and it was all sawed in half because they'd decided they wanted smaller amplifiers. I swear to God, there were all these half amplifiers lying around looking as if they were embedded in the floor.

At first we paid our share of the rent. After a while we didn't have any money, but we stayed on anyway. Month after month they got more pissed off, but thankfully they didn't throw us out. One night we got there and the elevator wasn't working so we had to climb fourteen flights up to our floor. When we got there we looked down the stairwell and some people were holding the elevator. We started cursing them out, shouting and fighting up and down the stairwell. They were talking real tough to us, saying, "You come down here!" We were screaming back, "Fuck you!" Then we all stormed and huffed into our rehearsal room. Later we found out they were robbers in the act of ripping off a company that made leather jackets, and that they probably could have come up and shot our faces in.

Around this time we started getting gigs at White's Pub. As I was a barmaid there, from time to time they mercifully gave us gigs in the afternoon playing for drunken business executives. We set up on the floor.

We rehearsed with Clem and Fred for a couple of weeks, then went out and did out first show as Blondie at CBGB's. This was our jungle night show, with me, Tish, and Snookie dressed as jungle girls in leather skins tied with thongs and accented by bits of fur. In between sets Fred freaked Chris out by telling him he was going to replace Hell in Television over the weekend. Chris realized this probably meant he was going to leave us because Television offered him a much better opportunity. They were beginning to get very good press, whereas we were being laughed at if noticed at all. Our second set was pretty bad as the sleazy realization that Television might be taking our bass player away crept in on us. We'd relied on Fred for a long time. He was/is a good musician, why else would they want him? What a blow to our prestige.

After Fred quit, we got very paranoid. We felt everybody in the scene was against us, and stayed depressed for a month. We threw up our hands and said, "What's the use? It's too ridiculous, this is really hard." Losing hurts. So we didn't do anything for a while. I auditioned for some "Top Forties" bands to try to make money while the two of us were on our own. I learned the Chaka Kahn songs then so popular. Finally Clem, whom we barely knew at the time, called up asking, "Are you going to do something or not? I think you should at least try." Chris

said, "Well, we have to get a bass player, it's practically like starting over." I was still working at the bar but we didn't want to talk about bands for a while. We were fed up and embarrassed with everything.

Blondie has always been a roll of the dice. Many times, early on, I made decisions by a roll of the dice. With only the two of us left in Blondie, we had to decide whether to chance working another year, possibly never getting anywhere. What was in it for us? We didn't have any money; we didn't have any outside means of support, except for some small bits of cash from Chris's mother. What else could we do but try again?

Around the end of '74 The Miamis threw a party at their house with Eric Emerson, The Dolls, Television, The Ramones, and a hundred other people all in bands. It was the last time everybody from that period was together. Shortly thereafter, Patti Smith started gigging with Clive Davis and Arista backing her up, The Ramones signed to Sire, and Television was considered worth signing by several labels—thus escalating the whole scene into an intensely competitive serious game, bringing to an end our short-lived camaraderie. The record companies definitely helped split everything up. The A&R executives who came around caused a lot of competition by concentrating on one group, which made everybody else get nervous. They were never interested in building up the whole scene. I remember that when Television broke up they had a big struggle, and Hell and Lloyd began to flake out. We went to see them at Max's once and both Richards were lying in fetal positions, unconscious, in opposite corners of the dressing room.

Malcolm McClaren owned an English boutique and for a while in the early seventies hung out with Rick and Liz Derringer, David Johansen, and various rock people in New York. His clothing store in London, called Let It Rock, sold fifties Teddy Boy gear, and The Dolls had picked up on it and him quite a bit. McClaren hung around for a while and picked up on managing The Dolls. He was the guy who arranged those red leather concerts at the Hippodrome that were some of the best shows they ever did and sold out every weekend for a month. The first weekend they played, the opening group were the rich kids we shared our rehearsal space with. They were backing up, with the most horrendous music imaginable, a Jobriath/Bowie concept show about being born out of a papier mâché egg and going through life. The only thing I can say for the rich kids is that when they came on at the end and did a song alone, they got a better response than the Jobriath clone's whole show.

The next week Television opened for The Dolls. Soon after that The Dolls went down to Florida with McClaren to begin a tour, and about twenty minutes later we all heard that Johnny Thunders and Jerry Nolan had left the group, flown to Paris, and that was that. Another twenty minutes later we all heard about The Sex Pistols, who, coincidentally, looked like a combination of Television and The Dolls. You have to hand it to Malcolm, he's got an ace sense of show biz. Although I don't think it's that hard to do

Ten performance shots.

that sensationalist stuff. The Sex Pistols were certainly conscious of show business, but for some reason everybody thought that just because they said "we're selling out," that makes it hip to do so. They were certainly conscious of what they were doing on a sensationalist level.

Brains and determination are what keeps bands together, but it all depends on the band, because each band has a chain of events that forms it, and makes it or breaks it for them, and they're obviously all different.

Personally I then felt so deep at the bottom of the scene that I couldn't imagine anybody being competitive with me. Blondie wasn't getting any reviews. I earned more money as a barmaid at White's, where Anya Phillips also worked briefly, than from working with Blondie in a club. Around this time we wrote "Die Young, Stay Pretty," "Heart of Glass," and "Live It Up."

Clem kept telling us we were good, that we had something. I never asked what "something" was, but he got us rehearsing again and began to bring a bunch of his friends from Bayonne around. Gary Valentine was the ringleader of these kids and pretty soon he started playing bass. If Clem was the Keith Moon of Bayonne, Gary had to be the Bob Dylan. He was super handsome and everybody in Bayonne knew Clem and Gary had to be in a rock group. Also from Bayonne came Ronnie Toast, a general inspiration during this period, who wrote lyrics and poetry. He was called Ronnie Toast because he accidentally burned down his parents' big house in New Jersey. After the fire he went back and wrote TOAST in spray paint on the wall. The people from the bug house apparently chased him down the street with a net. After that Toast was in and out of the bug house a few times. There was another kid called Crash or Prash, and assorted zombies on thorazine. Half of them were just burned out acid cases, which may explain why they were so attracted to us.

One of these kids kept having to go back to Jersey to go to court, and that's how Gary and I came to write "X-Offender." It turned out this poor kid had run away from home and had a sixteen-year-old girlfriend who was a hooker. He had fallen under her influence and she had gotten knocked up when he was seventeen. Inevitably he turned eighteen and, since he was no longer a minor, was being charged with statutory rape. Meanwhile he was begging the girl to get an abortion—even earned the money and gave it to her—but she refused. The kid was technically a minor when he committed his crime, but had become an adult by the time he was ready to be charged, so he was being treated as an experienced sex offender, when his crime was definitely one of innocence. Richard Gottehrer, who produced the record, added the introduction in the recording studio so that it seemed to be about a hooker bemoaning her downfall brought about by the police.

When I split from the Stillettoes and decided that I wanted to do less schtick and more music, I dropped a lot of the more obvious theatrical things, but at this point we tried to think up as many tricks as we could. The sicker and funnier the better. Some of the props

we developed were great, though. I had a black Mortisha dress, a gold lamé dress, a couple of stupid wigs, a green day-glo cross, a wedding dress, and a fishbowl with a goldfish in it called Mr. Jaws. He died one night when Chris forgot to leave his night light on, but he certainly managed to help us through a few shows. I was developing the Blondie character. She wasn't quite there yet, but she was on her way.

Concentration is the most important thing a performer must develop. During one of the first gigs Blondie did at CBGB's with me singing solo, I was so nervous I forgot the words to all the songs because I put myself in the place of the audience to see how I looked, instead of intensifying further what I was there for. It was hard to concentrate at CBGB's because it smelled so bad. Hilly Kristol, the owner, kept dogs in the back and they used to shit and throw up indiscriminately. The kitchen was covered with grease, rats, flies, maggots, and shit too. This I suppose added to the down-home atmosphere, and wasn't surprising considering the sea of human waste that spread around the Bowery, where a common sight would be a can of regurgitated spaghetti that some bum had sloshed down for breakfast but had been unable to hold. There was definitely something doomed about CBGB's kitchen. In fact, we didn't really go into it that much for fear of seeing a hamburger that had been lying in the same spot since 1951. After a show everybody sat down at the bar and had another drink. It was around this time that people kept telling me to get out of rock'nroll because I was awkward, stiff, nervous, and self-conscious.

This is an article I wrote and published in the late summer of 1975 in *51* (a magazine which thought New York City should be the fifty-first state and folded pretty quickly):

I walked into CBGB's last Friday night at 2 A.M. The Bowery was thick with late night pollution and smog, a sea of sleeping winos, and broken glass.

Dee Dee Ramone spotted me through a Heineken Haze and slithered up wearing an electric purple pimp suit, a Jays T-shirt, ragged basketball sneakers and mirror shades.

Swaying slightly, he whispered in my ear, Oh Debbie, we just got signed; we're supposed to be going on tour. I smiled. I wondered: Will Success Spoil . . . Dee Dee is bass player to the Ramones, consummate, awesome, punk rockers extraordinaire. The handsomest of the group, Dee Dee resembles Marcello Mastroianni or Steve Canyon, speaks German (born Berlin), was a highly paid hairdresser for a while, is very charming, handsome and childlike.

The next day was ninety-seven degrees and I ran into Tommy Ramone, drummer and leader to the band, in front of Arthur Treacher's on Sixth Avenue. Tommy, I heard you got signed, I quipped. He flashed me his disgusted look, Yeah, we got signed to the space program, three sets a night on the next moon shot. I didn't take it any further; it was very hot.

But for a few exceptions the NYC rock scene is built on dreams and fantasy. Dreams of love and power, of polite fascism and opulent anarchy; the have and have nots; EEE, eroticism, eccentricity, and eclecticism. It is more than fitting that the scene has filtered down to one tiny club on the Bowery. The expansive thoughts of all concerned could never have been contained in anything

Blondie takes shape: Gary, Debbie, Chris, Clem.

larger or more plush. (Except for Sunday evenings with the Miamis at Broadway Charlie's, Miamis are not too tight with the manager of CBGB's.) The rock and roll sub-culture coexists easily with the wraith-like alkies; the angry young black men; with the emptiness and ruin of America's attics, basements, and secret corners. Places where the out takes and out casts collect. Poverty Marches On . . . What the Hell: A bass player (now with the Heartbreakers) with so much sex appeal it could lead anyone, male or female into groupiedom, revolution be damned.

As I hinted at, an occasional glimpse of success is not uncommon here at CBGB's house bar. Last Thursday played host to the magnificent men of Kiss, playing homage to their old friends The Harlots of 42nd Street, who were doing their best to entertain the natives. Other notable drop-ins were Mick Ronson (ohh) and Ian Hunter (ahhh) who surprised everyone no end, including the Fast who promptly set up and played a second hot set on an otherwise dead night at the rock palace.

A few of the Bowery denizens have succeeded in related fields. Fayette Hauser, Gorilla Rose and Tomata du Plenty, who are behind the scenes Holywood writers for the new nationally broadcast Manhattan Transfer TV show. I do mean behind the scenes. Gorilla and Tomata are so far behind the scenes they're still in NYC, but word has it that they'll be getting some fresh OJ off their own tree within the month.

Just One More Thing . . . The great tower of power moloch Mainman is closing up shop. Mainman pro-

duced some fabulous shows like Wayne County at the Trucks, FAME, and Bowie. So much for EEE.

In this very casual atmosphere we played CB's every weekend for seven months in a row. There was no competition. The Talking Heads showed up bringing the Soho art world element with money which certainly helped broaden the spectrum of the audience. For a while the CBGB's scene had its own magic. Blondie, Talking Heads, Televison, The Heartbreakers, and The Ramones all struggled to keep it together, sharing equipment and supporting each other. You really had to be there to understand. At the stroke of midnight everyone would start wandering in, breaking the atmosphere in the bar like a wino's cheap pint splintering on the sidewalk out front. Every band was unique and had something going for it. Each band had its own following. We eventually developed a small audience of bizarros. Among our groupies there were two big Spanish girls and two people with bald heads and sunglasses. They were strange, but that was always good. Anya Phillips was a regular at CBGB's in the early days, as was Arturo Vega, who wore a Mexican wrestling mask the whole time for the first few months we saw him. He was simply known as the guy in the mask. He later became lighting man and art director for The Ramones. Nobody ever knew what it was about Roberta Bayley that made her capable of being the buffer be-

27

Clem Burke.

tween CB's and the outside world. She was a very cute girl with an even cuter attitude and somehow she managed to fend off anybody who looked wrong.

Tony Ingrassia directed the gig called Wayne County and the Trucks. It was held down where the trucks are parked, next to the river in the West Village. This was one of the first shows with the band off to the side of the stage. Wayne was out front running around the stage in those crazy outfits.

CBGB's was really great. The whole place was filled with books like *The History of Sexual Assault* and *The Marine Handbook*. Hilly was a beatnik from the word go. He knew exactly what was happening and was always very encouraging, but he only had one line: "There's something there," he'd say, "I can see there's something there." If there was I'm sure he would have been the first to notice, because Hilly was getting divorced from his wife, so she had the house while he lived in the bar with the indiscriminate dogs. After a year or so he got an apartment around the corner. But Hilly was cool. Hilly was also so strong he used to have his own moving company, and once he helped us heave a piano up a long flight of stairs. There were eight of us on one end and Hilly on the other. Speaking of pianos, after the rich kids finally threw us out for not paying any rent we'd moved down the hall into a more stoned-out hippie's smaller rehearsal room, with one amplifier and two drums in

it. This rehearsal space was his big gig, but he let us crash there without paying anything. Then the rich kids were away for months and their place was all destroyed, so one day we took a player piano that they had and sold it for $50.00.

After a while we decided we wanted to fill out our sound a little more. Jimmy Destri hung out at CBGB's and we remembered him because he was the only one in the audience with short hair and a black suit. He had played with Milk and Cookies right before they went to England to make their first album, but just before they left the band told him, "You can't come," so Jimmy'd gotten a full time job and gone back to medical school. We knew his sister Donna and she told us he was a great keyboard player so we asked him to give it a try. The first gig we played together was at Mother's, which was a bar made into a small club on West 23rd Street across from the Chelsea Hotel, where everyone played at least once. At that time people dealt with bar owners instead of agents to book gigs. Everybody was out of tune but we had fun playing together; it just clicked. At that point Blondie was a real energetic band in which everybody was giving his/her own mini-concert without focus. We were still a mess, but we were getting more and more excited about playing together. When we first got Jimmy he was a nervous wreck from his job as an orderly in Maimonides hos-

BLONDIE

Gary Valentine.

pital in Brooklyn. There were always dead bodies lying around and people with knives in their heads running in and he would have to subdue them. He was a real young guy and he was being trained and programmed for this hyper existence working all night in the Emergency Room, so he was pretty hyper around that period. He often used to come straight from taking a knife out of someone's head at the hospital to playing a gig.

Soon after Jimmy joined the band we got banned from CBGB's for a couple of months because Hilly booked us in and then threw on four other bands and Gary yelled at him. I admired Gary for it, and it was funny because soon after that the rock crowd who'd never really come to see us began filling up Brandy's and Monty Python's, across from Hudson's Army & Navy Store on the corner of 3rd Avenue and 13th Street, the sleaziest hooker neighborhood. Sometimes we were jamming with various musicians too, including some weird old hippies. We had a black conga player named Stepanji, who's since disappeared. We once played a gig at Mother's with a flute player and two conga players. It had been easier singing in The Stillettoes and with the Banzai Babies when I could submerge my personality with the other girls' and didn't have to work so hard. On my own I had to put out more than ever.

If there was one, the Blondie concept was akin to comic strips. Chris was a collector, Gary always had his nose buried in comics, and from my point of view the idea of a drawing coming to life and stepping onto the stage had a terrific surrealness about it. I wanted to create this character who was primarily having fun, even though she was being maligned by her friends and her heart was being stepped on by various members of the opposite, or same, sex. Even if she was getting ready to jump off the Empire State Building, Blondie was going to have fun on the way down.

I never wanted to approach rock'nroll from a man's point of view, and being a solo rock singer instead of in a trio made this more difficult because it was really not done at that time. I was always in a position of setting a precedent, which, from my point of view, gave me a definite advantage. Even if I went onstage and did a direct ripoff of Jagger or Bowie, it would never come off as a complete copy because Blondie is a girl. The initial idea was to be desirable, feminine, and vulnerable, but a resilient, tenacious wit at the same time rather than a poor female sapped of her strength by heartthrob and unrequited love. Apart from the relationship to comic books, Blondie always thought pop—i.e., dance music, movie themes, and the strict attitudes of modernistic fifties design. We were definitely combining these ideas in rock'nroll, and I wanted the girl Blondie to be funny, too. Fronting an all male band, singing their lyrics too, my perspective was further broadened. I could sing a song that Jimmy Destri wrote about not wanting to be tied down by a girl, or a song by Gary Valentine, who had an eye for the tragic in love relationships, or Chris whose material is eclectic, so I had a wide spectrum to draw from. When Blondie did finally hop out on stage as a character she would try to be bisexual or asexual, and a lot of times she would see and do things from the point of view of a third person. Above all, she was energetic.

BLONDIE ON THE BOWERY

By August, 1975, having two apartments had become unnecessary because we were spending all our time on Thompson Street, leaving The Ramones to hold the fort on First Avenue. Thompson was smack in the middle of Soho when it was just getting chic to live there, so obnoxious rich people were coming down all the time. We were appalled by what was happening to the neighborhood and wanted to move anyway. One day I saw a bunch of bozos beating up a black guy, who'd supposedly snatched a purse, while everyone in the street stood around watching. "Wait!" I yelled. "Don't beat him up! Call the cops!" The neighbors had never liked us because of our weird clothes and green eye shadow, but after that incident the atmosphere definitely turned, and the next thing we knew somebody broke in and robbed us. They didn't take much (not much to take), but when the ceiling fell down shortly thereafter, we were convinced. This crazy artist-magician we'd met called Eduardo invited us to rent a floor of his three-story loft building on the Bowery three short blocks from CBGB's; it was time to move from Thompson Street, and Chris abandoned his war zone crash pad on First.

We had the first floor, Eduardo lived on the second, and, for the first few months the third floor was empty. The Bowery was unheated funk, but the space was heaven. There was enough room for Chris and me to live, rehearse, and run the complex business of booking Blondie. The building had fittingly been a sweatshop, a doll factory employing child labor, which accounted, we figured, for a lot of the inexplicable things that happened there other than those caused by the actual physical inhabitants. The place was packed with poltergeists. After the doll factory it had housed Louis DeSalvo's private club. There were bullet holes in the windows of the back room, which had massive iron shutters that could have stopped a tank, even though the front of the building was completely unprotected. A famous philosopher's girlfriend, who was a very nice lady in great shape, with the Lauren Bacall look, had originally let Eduardo have this great space, and he asked us to move in when she moved out. But about a month or so after we moved in he started a downhill slide. He would go into a fake biker number, which involved not washing for days and sleeping in a piss-soaked bag with his boyfriend Alex. He worshiped

piss and would piss into beer bottles, leaving half full ones all over his floor.

The cats, who moved from Thompson Street to the Bowery with us, were the first to suss out Eduardo's number. They just ran up to his floor and pissed and shit all over his drawings and paintings. He was a talented artist too and we liked his stuff a lot, but he was, like so many people who inherit money, incapable of doing anything with his own art. He was gone, but he was definitely an inspiration. He evidently inspired the cats too, but in their case only to greater heights of secret shitting and pissing. His floor of the house was basically a toilet. Despite this, our place on the Bowery became a center of action as the punk scene quickly began to develop.

First of all *New York Rocker* came out, edited by Alan Betrock, who produced our first demos and with whom we'd done various projects. He played an important part in shining some publicity onto the groups and keeping the whole scene exciting. Then near the end of '75 *Punk* magazine appeared and topped everything off. Editor John Holmstrom, and his living cartoon creature Legs McNeil, were two more maniacs running around town putting up signs that said *"Punk is Coming! Punk is Coming!"* We thought, here comes another shitty group with an even shittier name, but when we went out to the newsstand one day there was this new comic rock mag that everyone loved immediately; it was always funny, very hip, and had lots of good pictures. I remember walking from the 82 Club past Phebe's to CBGB's one night with Legs, who was decidedly drunk on screwdrivers and started leapfrogging the parking meters. He did them all but when he jumped over the last one he just went, Nnnnnnnnnwwwww-www bang! Landed on his head making such a loud cracking noise that everybody in the restaurant stood up and looked. But Legs got up, said "Aaaaaaa-hhhhhhaa! Aaaaah!" and we helped him down the street. I don't know how he kept walking he was so fucking drunk. *Punk* became an organic part of the whole scene, as it was the most interesting magazine in the world when it came out. It was very cool to be in it, too. Chris contributed photographs frequently after the first issue. John once put a leather jacket and sunglasses on Jonathan, one of the dogs at CBGB's, and interviewed him asking, "How do you like it down here?" "It's horrible," Jonathan said. "It stinks of dog shit." *Punk* was a lot sharper than the other fanzines before it eventually collapsed under financial and personal strains.

We used to get some of our clothes on the street. New York has gorgeous garbage sometimes. Leather jackets, suits, and boots could be found in excellent condition. As a matter of fact, the famous zebra print dress that I posed in for an early poster was originally a pillow case rescued from the garbage by Eduardo.

I was feeling great for the most part during this period. We hung out and got along well with most of the other people/groups on the scene like Richard Hell, The Heartbreakers, Ramones, Miamis, and Dictators. Most of them thought of us as an opening band and they thought I was cute, but never thought we'd get anywhere. I was still using props, like for

Debbie on the subway again.

First performance by Blondie.

Chris, Fred Smith, Ivan Krall rehearsing with Debbie.

"Kung Fu Girls" I had some nine-foot-high cartoon monsters Eduardo painted, which I kicked through, jumping à la Bruce Lee.

One night we were over at Eric's apartment working on a tape of "Heart of Glass" on his Teac four-track tape recorder, when he suddenly staggered out of the kitchen looking ashen. He looked even more distraught and sad when we left. Being satisfied drove him crazy in the end, because he had everything so he didn't care about anything anymore. He used to go out jogging every day, and did feats of physical endurance like strapping twenty-pound weights on each ankle and then bicycling up to the Factory. The next day we were sitting around the house just after we woke up when Barbara called with the bad news. "Oh, Eric got hit by a truck." He had been a good friend and inspiration to so many people. We didn't quite understand what had happened, but we went up to a party/wake held for him and saw a lot of people from the earlier glitter days. Eric's death definitely marked an end to the glitter period. We still miss him. I'm sure if he were around now he would be internationally successful. He was definitely way ahead of his time. It's too bad his music was never released, not to mention what a gifted actor he proved himself to be.

By the end of 1975 we had got the band together to the point where we could go out to perform. Then

Clem went to England for Christmas to visit his girlfriend Diane Harvey at Oxford. While he was there he called us collect from a phone booth in London to the phone booth in CBGB's and we talked about everything for an hour. Hilly didn't know anything about the call. Anyway, you can't do that anymore.

During the six weeks Clem was away we rehearsed and wrote new songs, hoping he would be back in time for us to do a New Year's Eve show. Clem didn't come back in time, so New Year's Eve 1975–1976 we didn't do a show. New Year's Eve was always a total bust for me as a kid. I never had a date, I always stayed home, bored out of my mind, watching the stupid ball on the Time and Life Building drop at midnight. Sometimes I would get drunk alone, or else at someone else's place babysitting. Traditionally the worst night of the year for me, New Year's Eve has now put Blondie to work in the oddest places. I felt it was very important to work on New Year's Eve.

One of the events that marked the real start of the New York punk social scene was Clem's arrival back from England with the first Dr. Feelgood album. We threw a welcome-home party for him on the Bowery. If there's one group that could take credit for giving direction to the New York scene, it must be Dr. Feelgood. Clem had seen them in London, and the fact that a band like the Feelgoods could pack the Ham-

Debbie in 1975.

Eric Emerson.

Eric Emerson.

33

Backstage, Mercer Arts Center.

Debbie in Zebra.

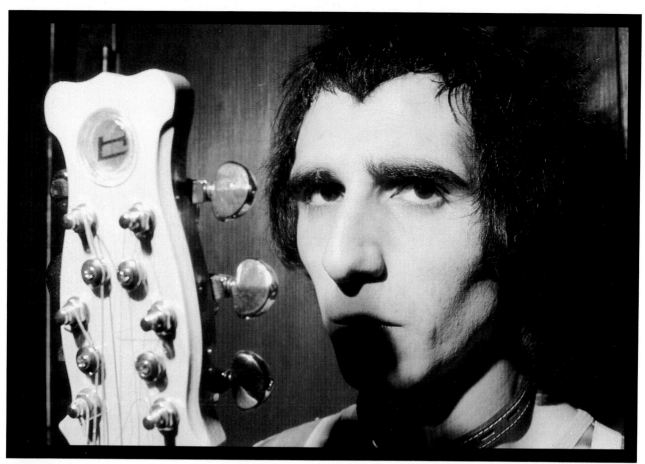

Miki Zone.

Debbie and Clem trying to walk down the street.

Mao Dead.

Debbie in Marilyn Monroe's burnt dress from the Seven Year Itch, in the burnt kitchen, 17th Street apartment.

Debbie and Clem in front of CBGBs.

mersmith Odeon and make it onto the British charts gave many New York bands conviction to keep on. Unfortunately Feelgood stayed together barely long enough to catalyze New York's bands before they broke up.

What a great party. Several hundred people came, stood around, and got fucked up. That was the first time Nancy Spungeon (who would later die in the aftermath of The Sex Pistols) showed up looking hot. There used to be a lot of great parties in those days where everyone would be in the same place at the same time.

We lived on the Bowery for a year surrounded by the symbols of our struggle. One time Clem and Chris went out to the store and rushed back in yelling, "Hey! There's a dead bum outside!" He was frozen in the snow. Somebody had seen him walking around in the snow with no shoes on earlier in the day. His eyes were open, he had a little white beard, and he had turned blue. Everybody ran into the street to look at the frozen bum until an ambulance came to scrape him up.

One bum we called Lon Chaney was always smiling. He would wear a top hat and pink overalls. Once he had on a pair of white men's longjohns, except they were all dabbed with paint à la Jackson Pollock or Larry Poons. Or he'd have on a military outfit. There was an abandoned storefront across the street

from us, where all the bums would crawl in and sleep. One day another bum came along with a big stick and commenced banging on the front of the place, and screaming for hours. The view out our front window often had the surreal look of a Fellini set, though the rotting decay of the Bowery was eerily peaceful after the local restaurant supply store closed in the evening.

The most important store in the neighborhood flourished on the street floor of our building. Mecca to the bums and winos, the liquor store was a busy place. The daily congregation of local residents naturally gave our downstairs hall the strong smell of piss too. Basically, we were trapped between two urinals. It was hysterical. We couldn't have a stove because there was no gas, and Eduardo wouldn't let us get an electric one, because there was a problem with the electricity. It was free and we didn't know where it came from. So we just had a hot plate.

Electricity, fire, and water gave us the most trouble. The pipes were always bursting, the fuses were always blowing in the middle of rehearsals, the place was dirty and it smelt terrible, so environmentally speaking we had it covered. One time Gary picked up a lamp and was instantly charged with 110 volts of current. Unable to let go of the lamp, he screamed for help. Chris knocked the lamp to the floor before Gary fried, but his arm hurt for days and he was pretty

Hot summer night.

Anya Phillips and Debbie in The Legend of Nick Detroit *by Legs McNeil, Punk Magazine.*
Artwork by John Holmstrom and Bruce Carlton.

shook by the event. Meanwhile we practiced every afternoon and evening, every day, every month the whole year. Chris and I were also managing the group, taking phone calls from ten in the morning until eleven at night.

If it hadn't been for the fireplace I'm sure we would have frozen to death, but the fireplace wasn't our only source of heat. The liquor store had a very old oil burner with a broken water pump in the basement. During business hours from eight to six the dear old burner chugged away, keeping us well toasted. But if someone didn't get into the store before six and fill the pump with water, the furnace automatically turned off. One extremely cold evening the store clerk said he had put the water in for us, which we thought was nice of him. However, at about four A.M., Howie, one of the fifteen extra people who lived with us on and off during our stay on the Bowery, was awakened by the cats. Howie woke Gary who woke us. Our nostrils were stained with soot, our hearts throbbing for lack of oxygen, and the entire loft was thick with sooty smog. It seemed that too much water had been added to the pump, causing an overflow that had put out the burner flame. Since the pump was still full and working, the sooty residue had been forced up the pipes, out the radiators, through the air, and into us! Oily soot covered every-

thing as we raced to open all the windows and doors. Meanwhile it was freezing, so Howie, Gary, and I sat in the car while Chris went around keeping all the windows open until the air was clear of fumes. We might have been dead in another half hour, but around five-thirty that morning, thanks to our perennial guardians, the cats, we were still alive to watch the sunrise.

Meanwhile things were continuing to develop. Danny Fields began a regular column in the *Soho Weekly News* and started giving some publicity to the downtown rock scene. Famous people started coming to CBGB's. Jackie Onassis was said to have dropped in one night, and it became very cliquish. The first time Danny wrote about us in his column was when we were in *Vain Victory,* a play by Jackie Curtis, which was made up of lines from old horror movies. Tony Ingrassia directed it. Blondie did the music and I played Juicy Lucy. This was an important move for us, introducing Blondie to yet another audience.

Money was still at a minimum and we did a lot of odd jobs to survive. I had quit the barmaid job because it was interfering too much with the group's schedule and I was tired of scotch and soda. Anya went on to become a photographer, then a stripper. I went into the belt buckle business, soldering stained-

Lester Bangs and Debbie on the beach at Coney Island in Mutant Monster Beach Party, *Punk Magazine.*

Same day on the Boardwalk.

glass squares into brass buckles for 50¢ to $1.25 each. I set up my workbench on the top floor, and for a couple of weeks the spooky noises, creaky floors, and total solitude increased my buckle production. But one morning, while I was soldering away, something pushed my hand as it held the hot iron. I continued soldering on the first floor. Our place on the Bowery was definitely haunted. Chris actually heard one of the little kids who worked in the sweatshop doll factory banging on the wall as he was painting it black one day, and caught a brief glimpse of him as he vanished.

On July 4, 1976, we drove back from Boston and arrived in New York at seven-thirty in the morning. We returned our rented station wagon uptown, then traveled downtown on a bus. We were bleary-eyed, stoned out of our brains, and fucked up from doing this big gig the night before, and the bus was full of these bright-eyed chipper old ladies wearing red, white, and blue American pinafores, who'd struggled in from Missouri to see the ships. When we got back to the Bowery we found a three-hundred-pound bum taking a two-hundred-pound shit on the front step. We took it for a genuine Bowery Bicentennial Welcome. Masses of patriotic tourists strolled through town all the day as we watched the boats and walked around. The Bicentennial was reminiscent of Goddard's movie *Weekend*. There were throngs of people

thronging all day long, like a big ant colony. And then we went up to parties in the last building Eric had lived in.

Eduardo's boyfriend Alex was a really sweet guy who was also fucked up on biker imagery. He had long hair, a blond beard, big muscles, and looked like a biker but used to go off five days a week to a normal computer job. He'd come back in the evening, put on biker drag, and sit in the piss-soaked loft smoking huge joints of angel dust after work. Then Eduardo would come home and he'd smoke two big joints of angel dust too. I don't think they had to do anything else, because we did a little of the angel dust occasionally and it was different than the shit that went around later. It was more psychedelic. Once Chris had ESP and saw Chairman Mao in the cats. One night he took a joint of angel dust to CBGB's and dosed everybody, pretending it was a regular joint. It only took one or two hits to get you fucked up so you were hallucinating and didn't know what was going on. Although I must say, we don't think angel dust is too good. It's akin to smoking a plastic bag, or Elmer's glue.

Eduardo and Alex finally sucked another victim, Steven Sprouse, into their environment. Poor Steven moved all his shit in before he realized there was too much shit already and something was definitely wrong, when Eduardo just kept him up all night.

Debbie and Bud, *back on the beach.*

Quite coincidentally, if you believe in coincidence, Steven Sprouse was a young, unemployed designer/painter and he did live on the third floor for a while until he was half frozen.

Mod clothes were cheap in thrift stores, and Steve loved the "op" clothes of the sixties, too. Oh for pegged pants, narrow lapels and small collars! None of these items were for sale new in New York when Blondie started, so finding a supply of pointed shoes in mint condition was a major event that could eclipse finding King Tut's tomb, causing en masse pilgrimages to Hoboken. Everybody in the band got a short haircut around the same time. Gary was first. This was all part of the process of jettisoning the Stillettoes style and dressing Blondie in the mod mood. I had worn a pair of black shorts once and Steven said that this was the right look for me. He gave me a pair of thigh-high black leather boots and black tights to go with the shorts. So as soon as we got back into the black I was right at home, everything clicked, and the mini look just suits my figure as well as being comfortable for shows.

I asked Steve what his ideas on dressing people are and he said, "I just call it modern, almost a uniform, be it dress or suit. I think that's the future. We have less and less time to choose, so five outfits of the same thing is a good idea. It's hard to find clothes that aren't overdesigned, I don't like to see designers get carried away with whatever they're doing. Like putting you in minis was modern-looking to me. The sixties appealed to me for all that bright color and op art. I like bright colors in monochromatic use that become a backdrop for the person wearing them. Also whatever you wear should be a trademark, like *one* piece of jewelry. Clothes and art are synonymous and should evolve together but not distract from the wearer."

GETTING SIGNED

Marty Thau and Craig Leon, who produced the first Ramones album, started a new company called Instant Records. They had been sizing up a lot of the new groups and soon after The Ramones signed to Sire, Marty brought Richard Gottehrer to CBGB's. Gottehrer had written and produced "My Boyfriend's Back" for the Crystals, discovered the McCoys and produced their hit "Hang on Sloopy," and founded Sire Records (originally Bell Records) with Seymour Stein. They became interested in us, and proposed that we do two singles, with Richard producing, on the Instant Record label. So we went into the studio and recorded "X-Offender" and "In the Sun." Richard and Marty went straight to Private

43

Interior shot, Bowery.

Cats. From the top, Gregor, Sunday Man and Daniel.

Bullet holes in windows.

44

Debbie in Bowery office.

Early inspiration.

Ronnie Toast and Michael Singer.

On the roof of Radio City Music Hall during the recording of the first album, Blondie.

Stock, played the tapes for Howard Rosen, and convinced him to put it out as a single.

Meanwhile grim reality was settling in on the Bowery. The electricity started to go out, so Eduardo found a maniac called Mike at the Mike, who was a nice, good-looking guy, and he used to wire everything up in a primitive way. He was a cro-magnon retard who was very intelligent at the same time, but Eduardo thought he was a slave and attempted to make him act out a master-slave relationship. He was called Mike at the Mike because he was a big talker. He thought he was a DJ.

Eduardo was freaking out so much he couldn't handle himself anymore. Alex had moved in with two Irish setters they kept chained upstairs, who added to the shitting and pissing. Along with the cats, and Eduardo's personal bottles of piss, it was getting crowded. The angel dust must've gotten to them because one day Alex had a complete and total freak-out. He was on the top floor screaming his lungs out for about five hours, saying things like: **I SEE TOMPKINS SQUARE PARK MELTING! I SEE THE GHOST OF ERIC EMERSON!** We were actually scared because he was a big guy and we were sure he was going to go berserk on us, but he just kept screaming, which made him hoarse for days afterwards. He was normally a soft-spoken guy who stayed in his garage for days fixing motorbikes.

Apart from piss, dust, and having too much money he didn't know what to do with, Eduardo's main downfall was sugar. He would make a cup of coffee and put in eight tablespoonfuls of sugar. Two cups of this special brew, which tasted like lighter fluid, accompanied by a few Hostess Twinkies, made up his daily protein input. Finally he started freaking out. We'd be asleep and he'd come screaming into our room dragging a dog on a leash, lie down on the bed, and start ranting about God and the Devil. It didn't bother me that he was crazy. On some levels it was great and I was always amused by him, but as he disintegrated it became more difficult to put up with his increasingly unbalanced antics, plus the sudden invasion of our privacy and sleep.

By this time Eduardo and Alex had moved to the third floor, the second having become completely uninhabitable after he'd smashed a large mirror—an act inspired by his mirror complex with the Hells Angels, with whom he had a spiritual affinity.

Our single did absolutely nothing, much to Private Stock's great disappointment, because they were a Top Forties company. However, they decided to take a chance and put up the money to make a Blondie album, but first Frankie Vali, who owned a chunk of Private Stock Records, had to come down to CBGB's to check out the merchandise. That was another moment in the club's history, and ours.

Debbie and Chris in front of CBGBs.

Getting signed is exciting, but it's surrounded by a lot of hassles, because when somebody tells you you're going to make some money—it doesn't matter whether it's five hundred or a million dollars—trying to split it up is the hard part.

Everyone told us Private Stock was giving us a good deal and we should sign the contract. We were ignorant and couldn't afford a lawyer, because we were still considered the band least likely to succeed (and everyone was grossly surprised when anything did happen). That was our first big mistake, and I want to advise everyone starting a band never to sign anything—regardless of the situation or what you're told—without your own five lawyers. (One, God! One will do.)

Just before signing to make the album we appeared in Amos Poe's famous movie *Blank Generation*. He came over with a camera and filmed the boys pushing my Camaro up the Bowery. Even though all these things were happening, we still didn't have any money. Most of the time we had been getting $60 for a gig, now we were getting $200 for a weekend at CBGB's or Max's, but we still didn't feel as if we were making it yet. I was always consciously observing and appreciating things, but as far as having visions of success we've been realistic. We both have a tendency to play things down, so as not to build ourselves up and get disappointed, and there was no feeling that we were going to be successful at the time. Everybody thought we might make it as big as the Dolls.

It gave our egos a nice boost when we first started getting loyal fans, even though they were as strange a group as we were. I know I survived the hard times by being obsessed. Chris says he survived them through fear of becoming a cockroach. We were never touted as innovators, but we really had a terrific amount of feeling for our songs and lyrics. They meant something to us and we put everything into them we could.

We went into the studio to make the album with Richard Gottehrer in August, 1976. At the same time Eduardo finally flipped completely and threw us out of our Bowery headquarters. The situation there had become so horrible that I guess it was a good thing he made us leave. What bothered me most was that he kept saying how he was our dearest friend, but kicked us out just as we were about to start recording. I said, "How can you kick us out when we have to go into the studio all the time? We don't have time to look for a new place." But he just wanted somebody else to play with. He particularly disliked watching us do anything careerwise. We'd gotten too serious for him with our daily rehearsals and business meetings. However, to this day, he still goes around telling people his pacts with the Devil made us succeed.

Hilly.

We moved from the Bowery to the top floor of a brownstone on 17th Street between 6th and 7th Avenues. A private sanitation company came by every morning at two-thirty, making an awesome amount of noise and sleep impossible. Eventually we had to move the bed into the kitchen.

The man on the first floor was a Eubie Blake type piano player named Mr. Brown. He was also a therapist for the Department of Social Services and one of his patients was a suicidal pyromaniac who used to crash in our hall. Up on the roof we found a mat covered with blood where he had butchered a squirrel or something, surrounded by chips of wood that looked as if they were meant to start a fire.

Gary had been living with us at the Bowery for six months. When Eduardo kicked us out he moved in with his girlfriend, Lisa Perskey, who has since become a successful television actress. I remember the first Christmas we were there everybody except Gary went away. He stayed all alone sitting there freezing in this huge loft, reading books on Nietzsche.

Blondie was recorded August–September, 1976, at the Plaza Sound Studio, in Radio City Music Hall. The dark cavernous room, built for Stravinsky, is suspended from the superstructure so it's vibration free. On the same floor as the recording studio are two rehearsal rooms for the Rockettes. The entire chorus line can dance, the orchestra can rehearse,

and no noise or vibration will reach the Music Hall. Plaza Sound had excellent equipment and engineers but has since gone out of business.

Turning sound into electrical impulse can be tiring. We usually worked from noon until one or two in the morning, six days a week, until the end when it was round the clock to finish by deadline. Richard produced at a very relaxed pace, trying to capture the inspiration in a song rather than get the perfect rendition. Learning to play and sing with headphones on is an accomplishment in itself, to say nothing of putting more than notes and beats down on tape. But learning to play for recording cleans up your act. In addition you learn to listen better, which makes playing live a hundred percent better.

First albums are the easiest to do because everyone knows the material inside out. The concept of that first album was based on the personality Blondie brought to the subject matter. When you listen to the whole thing you notice a predominant theme of violence and gunfire. I don't think there's a song without a reference to someone getting shot, stabbed, degraded, or insulted. It's prime time television on record.

Making our first record was fun, although it was a little frustrating because Richard kept taking vacations. Ronnie Toast wrote the lyrics for "Rifle Range" and some loose poetic notes from which we

Debbie rips off Cousin Bruce Morrow's T-shirt.

pulled the back cover copy. We liked Ellie Greenwich because of all the songs she wrote and Gottehrer knew her so he got her to sing some backups. When we finished the album in September we had a party in the studio for a few bands—The Miamis, The Ramones, Richard Hell, and the crew from *Punk*. Private Stock decided to hold up release until January of '77. We were still playing around New York in the clubs and continuing to do whatever we could to promote Blondie. We played a minifestival at a place on Second Avenue called the Quando Gym, a former church building now owned by the city and leased by a Puerto Rican neighborhood group. There were a couple of other bands, ourselves, and The Dictators were the headliners. We stole the show because everything was running very late, so we went on at two-thirty which was exactly the right time. We finished the set with "I'll Be a Big Man in Town" by the Four Seasons. After we played everyone started leaving because it was four in the morning. That was the first time I felt really good after playing. Super Heaven. Perhaps it was because that was the first real stage we played on, even though the place was decrepit and there were gaping holes in the walls that went all the way through the courtyard. Afterwards The Dictators and the promoters were pissed off with us for leaving them with no audience.

The next time I began to feel things were going to take off for us was that fall when we did a show at Max's. We had met up with a German girl called Gabi who was an actress. She couldn't get a green card so she had a hard time getting work, but she had terrific connections in Germany where she was a successful television star. We got friendly and she said she wanted to sing with the band at CBGB's in a special show for German television. Everybody in the band thought it was a waste of time because she wasn't a rock'nroll singer; but the money made it a must. We rehearsed "Starfucker" and "Bilbao Song," a cabaret number by Brecht. I sang the English part and she sang the German part. I even played drums on one of these things. After we finished we got paid by the television people, which was exciting, plus we had this German song added to our repertoire.

Also in September we started getting a little bit of notoriety and did a show at Max's, opening for The Heartbreakers. I walked onstage in the zebra dress, did the Bilbao song, and the audience went wild. It was the first time that this had happened to us, and that picture by Bob Gruen has been around the world a million times. After that gig we began to gain some balance, whatever we did now somebody was there to approve.

The first New Year's Eve that we worked was '76–'77, playing an outdoor show for the New York City Department of Parks. It felt like eighteen degrees be-

Debbie and Ellie Greenwich.

low zero, it was sleeting, raining, snowing, and there were six inches of slush on the ground, but we played anyway right in the middle of Bethesda Fountain in Central Park. There were four klieg lights at the top of the Grand Staircase, searching the cloudy skies. The trees were ice-coated, and everything seemed covered with crystal. There were about two thousand people there, and we earned $1,500. It was the most money we'd ever made. The Parks Department had four or five men dressed up as eight-foot-high white hands, and at the stroke of midnight, these hands of Time came marching down the staircase with the klieg lights shining on them. As soon as we realized what was happening, the band went into "Time is Tight" by Booker T. As the ball fell on Times Square at midnight Joel Siegel put us on his TV show playing in the background. I wore a silver minidress over thermal underwear and a fur coat. No matter what the boys wore, it's impossible to play with frozen fingers. The icy look was phenomenal. One of those moments that is xeroxed on my brain.

Blondie was released in January, 1977. At that time the only new wave bands that had put out albums were Dr. Feelgood and The Damned in England, The Ramones, Patti Smith, and now Blondie in the States. The next day we opened for John Cale at My Father's Place in Roslyn, Long Island, with Chuck Barris's song "Palisades Park." We got a great reaction from the audience and the press, even though they hadn't had a chance to hear the album yet, so things were definitely picking up.

Blondie got good reviews in New York. Everybody was surprised at how much more together the sound was than it had been only six months earlier. Proving that the more you do something the better you get. By the time the record came out we were less nervous, had a better rapport with one another as a group, and I knew what I was doing with the music so that I could get more out of the performance. Our first album was recorded at an early stage of our development; we'd only been playing together for nine months. It took all our energy to write and arrange material and get it together to present. Technically we had a lot to accomplish. The biggest problem we had was learning the record biz. We had a production deal with Richard Gottehrer and he made the album and sold it to Private Stock, who were primarily interested in doing singles deals, and not artist development. For example, the Debbie Harry see-through blouse solo poster the record company put out as promo for the record was a fiasco, and insulted the rest of the band considerably. We all told them a group pic would be preferable and asked them not to put it out.

At least we were definitely on our way. When Rodney Bingenheimer called us up at 17th Street to

Richard Hell and Debbie.

Joey Ramone and Debbie.

Early Ramones.

interview us for L.A. radio, we thought it was a big deal. He was playing our record out there. He'd seen Chris's "Cream Dream" centerfold of me in *Cream* Magazine so he was saying, "Oh God, how old are you?" Hoping I was a teenager.

After he made the first record, Richard Gottehrer ran into Peter Leeds, who had been my manager when I was in Wind in the Willows. At one point Richard expressed interest in managing us, but we weren't interested in a producer/manager deal and he knew it. He reintroduced me to Leeds. I was not fond of Peter, but he was the only one who came to us and said "I want to manage you" who had a suit, a good pair of shoes, and a nice house. He also told us if we signed a contract with him we could get out of it easily if anything went wrong.

Since Private Stock was free to treat us any which way, we were very keen to get management. By February, 1977, when we went to L.A. with him, we had agreed that Peter Leeds would be our manager and he was having the contracts drawn up.

His idea was for us to establish ourselves in L.A., which made sense. Leeds put us in the Montclair Dunes Hotel where he'd arranged for us to pay the rent by playing a gig at the owner's disco. He of course stayed at a much better hotel.

Going to L.A. was a big deal for us at the time. We played the Whiskey for a week and blew everybody

including ourselves away, then we got another week with The Ramones and that was also a big success. Everybody in L.A. was ready for us, as nothing was happening out there at the time. They had all been hearing about us via Rodney, who'd been pushing us on the radio, so they were curious and the shows were sold out.

Phil Spector came to see us wearing an In The Flesh button and subsequently invited us to his house to discuss the possibility of producing our next record. He trapped us in one room for a while. We couldn't move around. If you stood up he wanted to know where you thought you were going, but I love nutty people and I'm really attracted to them. I sang some songs, Chris played guitar, and Phil was interestingly like the Magic Christian.

Mike Chapman also came a couple of nights in a row and he enjoyed the show. He thought that we were hysterical. He couldn't get over my plastic sunglasses, plastic purse, and polka-dotted miniskirt. He was giggling away. I guess it brought back memories to him. He communicated to us that he liked our material and was available to produce us. Malcolm McClaren was also hanging around the Whiskey but The Ramones didn't like him and when Malcolm made some remark Johnny said, "Are you talking to me?", jumped up, and chased him out of the dressing room swinging his blue guitar at his head. Malcolm

Heartbreakers: Richard Hell, Johnny Thunders, Walter Lure, Jerry Nolan.

beat a hasty retreat. We had a great time.

This was, however, also the scene of our second big mistake: signing a managerial contract with Peter Leeds. None of us had any money or knew what was going on, and he told us if we didn't sign the contract he was going to go home and leave us in California. Though I must admit he did arrange for us to have legal consultation on that deal. We had a half-hour conference with Private Stock's lawyer Howard Wattenberg, who told us if we trusted the guy to sign with him. Ironically enough the only reason we had any connection with Peter Leeds in the first place was because he had been my manager.

At the time we didn't think we had anything to lose or gain. I imagine it would have sounded completely ridiculous at the time if Leeds had told us that he thought we would one day be huge and make millions of dollars. Our situation was fucking horrible. We had to beg for money for shoes or clothes. One reason we finally had to terminate Leeds later on was because he always treated us like children. Everybody was hard up financially even when we were beginning to be a success.

Anyway, Chris, Gary and I went over to his hotel. Gary really didn't want to sign the contract and was flipping out with the adolescent shakes. Leeds was staying in a suite at the Sunset Marquis, so when we trooped in we thought, shit, reflecting upon our lousy

rooms at the Montclair Dunes. Much to our later chagrin, we convinced Gary to sign anyway because Leeds repeated that if anything went wrong, or we didn't get along, we could get out of it real easily. He told us everything would be cool, and like the fucked-up idiots we were we believed him.

Business is one of the most difficult things to deal with emotionally. You don't think there's an evil man with a cigar lurking around the corner. Even when you have it confirmed as a reality you still can't believe it. But people have to work this out for themselves and actually see all the clichés come true.

Blondie was the first of the New York bands to play the Whiskey, plus our visit had a definite effect on the L.A. fashion scene. When we arrived, most kids were wearing bell-bottom pants, but by the end of the first week girls were wearing miniskirts, while the boys were suddenly packed into straight-legged tight pants and sporting skinny ties. We brought the mod look back to L.A. They completely loved our look which was easily available in hundreds of thrift stores at the right price, real cheap.

We were having late night parties at our hotel and one night Jimmy and Clem got into a fight with another guest, who couldn't handle it anymore because we were making noise in the hall while he and his old lady were trying to go to sleep. He came running out of his room swinging and a big fight ensued right

Ramones play CBGBs.

Fred Smith, Debbie, Dee Dee and Janet Planet.

Very early Ramones.

Wayne County before doing a benefit.

Heartbreakers play CBGBs.

The Miamis.

Ramones play CBGBs.

Claudia and Tommy Ramone.

Very early Tom Tom Club: The Weymouth Sisters.

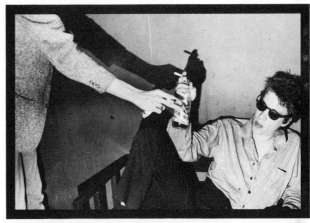

Richard Hell's last gig with The Heartbreakers.

Dee Dee Ramone with fans and friends outside CBGB.

Same.

Very early Ramones.

Tish, Debbie, Snookie.

Hotel Bar: Debbie and Nancy Spungeon.

Richard Hell's last gig with The Heartbreakers, Max's.

58

Debbie in Hollywood.

Two members of The Avengers.

Kim Fowley.

Joan Jett.

Debbie distracts driver.

Debbie about to be run over.

Cheri Currie.

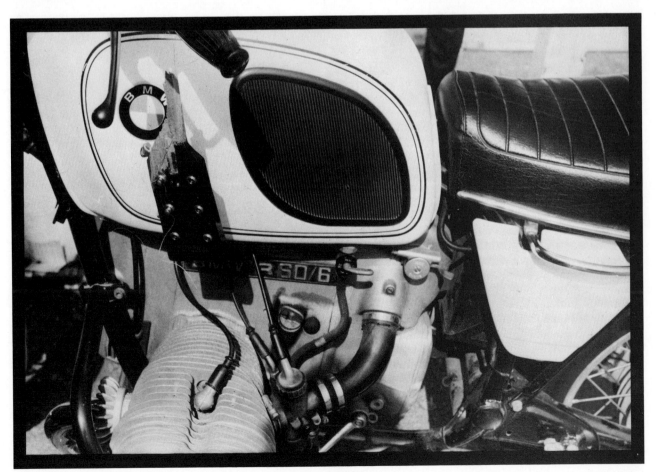

The head of Jimmy's broken guitar hangs from Bruce Patron's motorcycle.

Debbie with shades.

Debbie with bike.

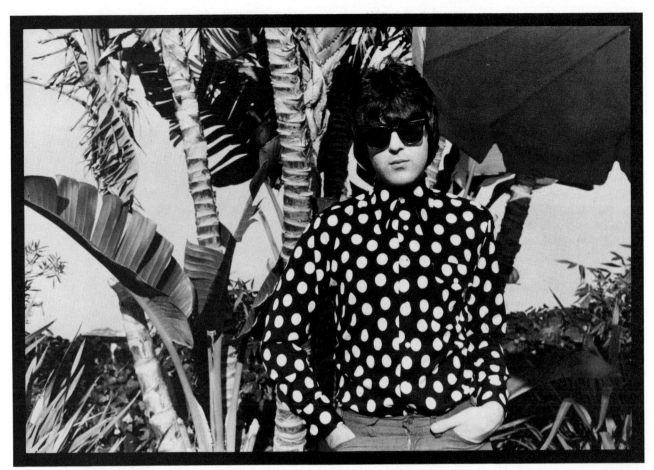

Clem blends in with the environment.

Hotel life.

Screamers: Tomata and Geaer.

Ray Manzarek and Debbie.

Debbie, Suzie Quatro, Joan Jett.

Gary, kid, Debbie, on the strip, L.A. (Note date on poster.)

Debbie and Iggy.

there, during which he grabbed Jimmy by the hair, dragged him around the floor, and began jumping on him. Finally the police came making the madness official, and especially infuriating the hotel management. They moved us up the hill to nicer rooms with great pink kitchens that night. The whole hotel arrangement ended as a write-off for the poor owners of the Dunes.

They were in control of a landmark disco in L.A. but hadn't wanted to pay the previous owner's electricity bill, so had set up their own generator which had the wrong wattage and output. During the first or second big gig they held, all the light bulbs blew out of their sockets. The electricity went off and there were a thousand screaming punk kids inside the disco. That's where we were supposed to play, but after they blew it up they decided to set up the gig on Catalina Island. They planned to ship two thousand doped-up teenagers to this bucolic little island. Obviously they didn't get permission, so that was that: the gig never materialized. It was a chaotic time.

When I began doing shows I tried to avoid the hackneyed rock poses and movements, along with the usual use-me-abuse-me attitude of most girl singers mentioned earlier. I don't try to come on too tough either. Like in "Heart of Glass" I say that once I had a love and it meant everything and I threw myself into it, but then it didn't work out. I don't pretend

not to care, that's the biggest front going. So the whole business is a pain in the ass. It's also a pain to have to feel pain.

While we were in L.A. we got word that David Bowie and Iggy Pop had heard our album in Berlin and wanted us to do the Iggy tour. After playing clubs in New York only twice a month, the positive response we got in L.A. and now this invitation to tour with two of our greatest heroes popped the top. When we got up off the floor Leeds informed us that he'd also booked some more gigs for us in San Francisco. We went up there and played the Mabuhay Gardens, where we put the first graffiti on the walls in the dressing room. Nice clean walls when we arrived, but now they're obliterated with layers of graffiti. After three weeks on the West Coast, Blondie came home to New York at the beginning of March to get ready for our first tour of the States.

THE IGGY TOUR

On Friday, March 11, 1977, we played a midnight set and a two A.M. show at Max's Kansas City, and then got into a stupid Winnebago mobile home and drove 376 miles to Montreal, Canada, where we stayed at

Hotel life.

the Manor Le Moyne. It was raining and cold when we arrived. On Sunday, March 13, we played our first concert with Iggy. We arrived at our dressing room and all of a sudden Iggy and David appeared. We hit it off right away. Iggy and David accepted us as working musicians, treated us as pros, and gave us a sound check at every show. They were relaxed and helpful and we certainly learned a lot from them. David would come out, prop his head in his hands right in front of us, and give me suggestions on how to improve my performance. He was willing to help. It was a great thrill to meet them and a pleasure to work with them because they were both so polite, friendly, encouraging, and well organized throughout the tour. The whole show was important as they saw it, not their half alone.

At this time we felt that radio was pretty stale. Everything on the American scene had been cooking in its own juices for years. Groups had broken into splinter groups and those splintered into millions of other groups, so it was the same people doing the same stuff. It seemed as if nothing had happened on radio in ten years. We wanted to entertain people with good music more than give them an attitude or philosophy, and all our songs were fast and different yet they all sounded like us. Our first album, which we were intent on delivering during this tour, was a calling card.

After Montreal we played Toronto, Boston, New York, Philadelphia, Cleveland, Detroit. We didn't party out much with Bowie and Iggy, because Bowie wasn't flying so he'd always be driving, which took him so much longer to get from one place to another that he would just go in his room to sleep. Iggy was always running around looking for something to do. Still there were a couple of parties. . . .

There's a super strong Iggy cult in Seattle. Some guys came up and asked us how they could meet David and Iggy. They told us they were having a party and that we should try to get David and Iggy to come. Clem, Jimmy, and Gary had told Iggy about it but he said he didn't want to go so they went without him and there were all these kids hanging around; you could tell they worshipped Iggy.

All the walls had Iggy graffiti on them like "Iggy is God." They were there for about an hour when all of a sudden the door opened and Chris walked in with Iggy, who sat down and started holding court surrounded by fans. They were in this tiny room with these funky amps and a small stage that was made up of a board on a mattress and bounced around as the musicians played on it. That was one of the best times on the tour.

These kids that couldn't play were playing when Iggy jumped up on stage and wound up singing for forty-five minutes. The Blondie boys played too.

Debbie and Iggy.

Jimmy.

Iggy and Chris.

Downtown, Someplace, U.S.A.

They did "Backdoor Man," and "Gimme Shelter." Iggy wouldn't do his songs, but he did MC5 songs, and anything that came into his head, a lot of improvisation. It was a small room with fifty people piled in. He took off his shirt. These people were devoted to Iggy and he hadn't been around for so long. Apparently the feeling in the room was amazing. These were kids who probably didn't know about his records when they first came out, but had them all by now. Afterwards he got down with a speech about how the kids were so young, they shouldn't get themselves screwed up, and then he said it was the best he ever sounded.

From Seattle we went on to Portland, Vancouver, and San Francisco. After three months on the road you go sort-a-crazy. We were invited to a party in San Francisco with the Tubes. Jimmy, Gary, and Clem got there late. They went up to the door but the bouncer wouldn't let them in because it was too crowded. They told him they had been invited but he still wouldn't let them in. Clem kicked the door and the bouncer started chasing him. Jimmy walked up to the door—two solid sheets of plate glass—and stuck his foot through one. The host wanted to put a contract out on him. In the ensuing scuffle Penelope, who was later in The Avengers, jumped on someone and bit his arm, enraging him to the limit. Bowie paid for the door and saved Jimmy's life, but later the guy who'd been bitten apparently took out a contract on Penelope, because during an Avengers gig somebody ran up on stage and bit her.

Friday, April 15, we wound up the Iggy tour at Santa Monica Civic Center. That tour was the best way to begin our touring career. Looking back on how professional David and Iggy were always made me feel much better when we later toured with amateur creeps who gave us a hard time. Meanwhile Leeds was scheming up our first overseas package tour of England with Television's manager Jane Friedman.

Before going back to New York Blondie played another week at the Whiskey. The last gig we'd done on the Iggy tour, we had been joking around with Tony and Hunt Sales (Ig's band) and invited them to put a band together to open for us. We said it as a joke, but a couple of days later they called to say they had a band together and could do a gig.

We wound up having a jam. We did "Anarchy in the UK" with Joan Jett and "I Wanna be Your Dog" with Rodney Bingenheimer playing keyboards. Joan played guitar and Tony and Hunt Sales were in on it. Clem was singing lead and I was his dog. He had me on a chain. Hunt came over from the side of the stage and jumped on Clem and started fighting him for the microphone. Rodney was concentrating on this one note on the keyboard like John Cale. We had written

Debbie and Bowie.

where he should hit. These final gigs at the Whiskey at the end of April were a culmination of everything that had happened, but they only represented the tip of the touring iceberg.

Back in New York we took stock of our situation. We were thinking about who should produce our next album and hoping we might be able to work with Bowie. We loved *Low,* which had just come out, and during the tour we'd found he liked a lot of the same stuff we did, like Kraftwerk and genuine German neoimpressionist dada muzak. One thing we'd noticed was that when we played in New York at CBGB's and Max's, which were the only places we could play regularly in the Spring of '77, we didn't see many teenagers. The audience were all professional music and art people or college students. When you get out of New York the audiences are largely high-school kids. Younger kids aren't so preoccupied with being cool and naturally fall into things. They are cool or they aren't cool. They're more aggressive too. At the Whiskey teenage kids in tons of leather and metal didn't give a shit whether they were cool or not, they just did it. A prime example of the contained attitudes of a lot of the people in New York is what happened the night Lester Bangs made his rock debut. It was hysterical. Lester thought he was a three-hundred-pound Jim Morrison. It was an event like nothing you ever saw. They destroyed the fucking stage. Legs McNeil was up there. He got hit in the balls with a pickle. They threw the piano over. Lester was doing a semi-religious number. I was laughing so hard my face hurt. Then I looked around and the critics in the audience were analyzing away, thinking, "Bangs brings a new austerity to minimalist rock bla bla bla." They had no idea what was so funny. However, Lester does have a good voice.

People were saying that Blondie's sound had gone from awful to terrible in a very short time. It's amazing what decent equipment will do. Some bands fucked up more times than I can count and the others would do three songs and walk off. I didn't get it. We were hardly received in New York for a long time and we didn't sound very different. It was just like The Runaways. People see a chick and . . . Really! We thought The Runaways were great and there were numerous bands who were worse. The reason they were being put down and others weren't was that they were cute "vulnerable" girls who weren't managed right. The press stomped them mercilessly. If they had been boys it definitely wouldn't have happened to them.

I think all kids should concentrate on being in rock bands or sports etc., to be themselves and try to gain power and get famous. The world would be a better place. Instead of getting high and being frustrated, kids should focus their energies. Kids during puberty are going through a tremendous physical/chemical change, so it's like taking drugs anyway. Consequently if you take drugs when you're going through puberty they have an even stronger effect. Adolescence is such a tumultuous period you have to channel your energies. When you're a kid it's important to do something like be in a rock band, otherwise you get bored, get stoned, go nuts, and run around.

Some people come from good situations and others adverse ones. I suggest keeping the things that you value to yourself until you're in a position to use them. Don't go Blech. If you've got instincts inside you, and you're sixteen years old and can't express yourself or do the things you want to do, wait until you're eighteen. Obviously you have to be cool for two years. I know it's a drag because I had a lot of the same opinions and energies that I have now when I was a kid but I could never use them. It's brutally frustrating to think about all those years sitting in school like a zombie trying not to nod out while the teacher's talking about her views on socialism and you know that she's an antiquated jerk who goes home and privately hates niggers, Jews, fags, hippies, gooks, commies, etc. I don't advocate drugs or dropping out, but I certainly advocate changing the idea of school. If all the kids in the country didn't go one day and just said "Close it! We want our rights!" What would they do? Put them in jail?

In time we'll reevaluate education because all it does now is teach you how to memorize. There are so many more things the brain can do and that's what educators should be teaching. To close on a positive note I must say that a few of my teachers opened new worlds for me. And now with computer educational aids, specialization and progress can be determined individually, making learning a more personal experience.

The boys fighting.

Debbie shouting.

Chris, Clem, Jimmy.

THE PLASTIC LETTERS PERIOD

FIRST ENGLISH TOUR:
MAY 17–JUNE 3, 1977

The night before we left New York the Camaro got stuck in reverse on Avenue of the Americas at 34th Street. I had to back all the way downtown between lights pretending to be looking for a parking space. I backed into a garage and told the guy somebody would pick it up. I gave the car to Vinnie, another one of Clem's friends from New Jersey, who said he could afford to get it fixed. He was the one who originally got it stuck in reverse (due to a very fragile linkage) after he jammed the shift. I used to bless the car every time I got it into any gear. I'd coax it along, whispering, "Second gear, c'mon, oh yeah! *Very good*," praising it as I was driving.

When we stepped off the plane in London the next morning, Tuesday, May 17, 1977, we were psyched. The first couple of days in London we stayed up wandering around with our mouths hanging open, looking at architecture, thinking about Shakespeare, the Romantic Poets, and Carnaby Street. It's every American pop band's dream to tour England and we were mesmerized. We saw Wayne County perform at Dingwalls. He was running around screaming in all those different outfits. Later on I imagined Coleridge visited me in our garret room at a cheap hotel in Kensington, and I wrote this poem about it.

Lips painted part
passing breath
into your name.

The room was so small we couldn't walk past each other without one person having to sit on the bed. We didn't mind that, the problem was that the hotel had just been taken over by some Arabs who didn't know how to run the telephone system, so our manager and press agent Toby Mamis couldn't make or take any phone calls, which made it hard to do business. The press asked us how we felt about opening for Television. All they wanted to know then was were we punks. We told them we were musicians, but the responsibility of the press is to categorize and identify everything, so what we looked like meant something to them.

We also did an interview with *Sniffing Glue,* which was the big underground mimeograph mag of its day, and that's when we first met Eddie Dugan. He was a little kid who was very polite and pleasant. We thought he was going to be rude but it turned out the professional journalists were the ones who came in and snarled, "You're punks, aren't you?" Eddie came in and said, "Ooooh, look, it's you."

The tour officially began at the Apollo Theatre in Glasgow. We had a warm-up gig scheduled at a club called The Village Bowl in Bournemouth on the south coast, Friday night, May 20. A British band called Squeeze opened for us. The kids were wild, spurring us on. By the second set around midnight everybody was half-pissed and crazy. Being onstage in England was immediately different from playing in the States because the audience reaction was exuberant. Some kids even tried to drag me off the stage. This great gig psyched us up and we went charging on to Glasgow the next day, where we saw The Ramones and Talking Heads play a college. Everybody packed into the gym and the floor started buckling because kids were jumping up and down to the beat, throwing beer all over the place. Around ten P.M., when the show was over, it was still light outside because it's so far north. Some of the pictures in here are from that gig.

It was weird traveling around England feeling like you never left CBGB's. We checked into the Central Hotel. Television wasn't arriving until the next day. The headliners are in control of how much power, sound, lights, and time the opening band gets. In this situation bands either work together, like we did with Iggy and Bowie, or try to outdo each other. When we got to the sound check at the Apollo on Sunday afternoon we found our equipment pushed to the front of the stage, where Television wanted me to confine my movements to a small space so that their front person, Tom Verlaine, could stand strikingly and somberly alone in a very large space when he came on.

The Apollo is a tough place to play under any circumstances. It's a cavernous hall which holds three thousand people. The sound is echoey and horrible. The stage is fifteen feet high so the kids can't jump up and kill the performers if they don't like them. Five hundred kids came to the first show. Half of them wore plaid shirts, had long hair and beards, were smoking joints, and didn't know our name. They were simply waiting for Television. The other half were all wearing skinny ties and trying to rush to the front, but without ropes or ladders they couldn't assault the stage. The audience was clearly divided and confused. We came off feeling terrible.

The vaulted ceilings created the right atmosphere for the religious tones of Television's music. Our second set didn't go any better and we returned to the hotel wishing we'd played a club. Meanwhile, without informing us, Television's record company, which was richer and more prestigious than Private Stock, had flown the cream of the British rock press to the gig. Afterwards we sat in our hotel depressed and un-

Debbie takes off.

informed. Needless to say, the following day Television received raves, everybody said we stank.

To encourage the friendly atmosphere we traveled in separate buses. Every day we'd wake up, get in the bus, and drive to the next city. Meanwhile our relations with Gary Valentine were definitely breaking down. He wanted to play guitar, sing solo, and get a lot more of the spotlight, but the idea of the band had always been that I was the front person. It wasn't just Chris and I who had problems with him. He and Jimmy always used to fight. Gary was the Brian Jones of the group, pairing off with Clem and whispering his complaints. We always had trouble with him, and when we had to tell him to limit jumping around like Wilko Johnson from Dr. Feelgood he understandably resented it. However, we weren't fighting amongst ourselves as much as we usually did, having had to focus on our common increasing enmity with Television.

After Glasgow we played Newcastle, Sheffield, and Manchester. We had two roadies: Michael Sticca was an American punk who'd started out with The Dead Boys and Keith Crabtree was a ginger-haired Yorkshireman we picked up on this tour. Sticca was always getting into trouble. Crabtree was a family man who supported his wife and two kids, but he had such a heavy accent we could never understand what he was saying. He used to say "OI" the whole time. That was about all we could understand. They were both with us throughout our tour of the world.

Manchester was one of our best gigs and we began to get good press, which was a relief. I found the English music press more sophisticated than their American counterparts. The clothes I was wearing associated me with radical elements who were uptight with the government. On this first tour my image was abused and criticized one day, but raved about and complimented the next. We soon realized this is how they sell papers in England too and has nothing to do with how records are made or groups perform. I was also beginning to find English kids somewhat more literate and sophisticated than Americans. They clock everything and were catching all the nuances in the phrasing of the music and words I was singing. They appreciated our act right away, making Britain Blondie's second home.

Our initial attraction to England was based on the now largely nonexistent swinging London of the sixties. By the time we got there England was on the brink. Prices were high, taxes were higher, and even bored businessmen bitched about the cost of heating Buckingham Palace. The Jubilee to celebrate twenty-five years of rule by Elizabeth II was a bargain basement bicentennial. Most people were either on strike or the dole and the Rolls Royce fantasies of the sixties were gone forever. There was a pervasive

Gary and Clem, Glasgow hotel.

atmosphere of restless haunting discontent.

By the time we got to London on Saturday, Television must have been feeling the chill because the press were calling them the Ice Kings of Rock.

It was great being in England because everybody was breaking out in this blossoming punk period, rushing around and going to clubs. Private Stock treated us well but they didn't take us everywhere free in big cars. Punk hadn't materialized in that big a way yet. We were moved to Bailey's Hotel and this was when we began working on some of the material for *Plastic Letters*. "Detroit" was inspired by that first English tour.

We played two nights at the Hammersmith Odeon. I wore a black miniskirt, black tights, and black leather stilletto ankle boots, so I was hot to go. We did the songs from the album, plus "Jet Boy," "Detroit," "Heatwave," and "Little GTO," and had a great time.

Detroit-like sensibilities were everywhere—toughness, desperation, intense alienation. The place felt like it was ready to blow. The patterns of the American sixties were right there like a time warp. They even had their own little Vietnam War going in Ireland. The key to the set-up is the difference. The American protest movements of the sixties were inspired by comfortable middle-class college kids. The English kids of the seventies got jobs at seventeen if

they could, and certainly most couldn't afford to go to a university. Your typical English rock fan works all week, and gets bloody pissed every night with Friday on his mind. Style is the second key. There's still a lot of difference between England and America, but the cultural influences have been going back and forth for so long now that it's becoming unnecessary to ask where something began. The Ramones were a strong catalyst in England, but it's unfair to say English groups copied them. They didn't any more than Sam the Sham and the Byrds copied the Beatles. However, the difference between how the New Wave groups like the Clash, and the old wave, like Elton, Rod, Mick, or Paul, came off was extensive. The new wave was revolutionary, idealistic, poor, and romantic. The old wave was bored, debauched, foppish, and rich.

We were getting adjusted to playing in England and getting very turned on by our audiences. We also got great reviews. Television just continued with their somber approach and the press came down heavily in an extraordinarily quick turnaround. Even though we didn't realize it at the time, this turnaround was a prime example of the "build them up knock them down" approach taken by the press, which was happening to both us and Television in reverse. Sometimes the process takes years to manifest itself.

Liverpool station.

Debbie and Gary on the sight of the Cavern Club, Liverpool.

80

Liverpool station.

Gary and Debbie overlooking the river Mersey, Liverpool.

English tour.

Debbie in Glasgow.

I always liked our English fans a lot because they were so encouraging. Girls and boys came up to me and said, "Great. Keep going. Do it." Which is what I wanted to hear my whole life. We were communicating more directly to them than to our American audience.

They're subject to terrible boredom sitting in their parents' houses like prisoners. Fewer TV shows are aired. All they can do is rush down to the pub at eleven A.M., sip a pint of lager as slowly as they can, get completely knackered by noon, and stay that way until the pub closes at three. England is an unbelievably repressed country, but the anguish and violence this repression causes makes the kids more colorful than their less focused American counterparts, who have it much easier. The difference between the daily living situation of a white American and an English kid is enormous. Nobody in the world as a group has it as easy as white Americans.

Monday, May 30, Television stayed in London to do a TV show. We went down to Plymouth and played a show with the Cortinas. Tuesday we played Bristol's Colston Hall. Clem was acting up in the dressing room, sticking pieces of bread on his jacket instead of safety pins. He was just about to start putting mustard on the bread when we got called onstage. One time in England he took a wastebasket and dumped it over his head, then went down to the

desk with cigarette butts in his hair and cigarette boxes sticking out his jacket pockets, and asked for a car. We played the album plus The Doors' "Moonlight Drive" and "Detroit" at the gig. The kids went nuts. At the end of the show Gary walked right off the edge of the stage as he wasn't wearing his glasses, but we lifted him up, ran back out, and did "Little GTO" as an encore. The next day we drove back to London and spent a couple more days at Bailey's. We were beat by then so we destroyed our rooms and left—promising to return to wake the country up to our sound. We weren't going to let our passionate new English fans down.

We loved our first visit to England and always enjoy going back. However, on this first overseas tour our manager had booked us into halls when we should have been playing clubs. Our press agent had been too aggressive and American. He was always charging into these British offices throwing publicity pictures around trying to make a deal. He was too over-the-top for them. Television had behaved erratically. The press had been up and down, and we'd had, and still had, no money. These things combined created bad working conditions, and the overall effect was horrendous. Back in New York I went straight to bed to hide and it was a week before I could summon up the strength to peek out from under the covers again. Then Vinnie called to tell me he had had a

Hotel life.

friend tow my car to a junkyard for destruction. However, you cannot have a car destroyed in a junkyard without a bill of sale and Vinnie didn't have one, so they'd driven the '67 Camaro off a cliff. Feeling empty myself besides missing my wheels, I wrote "I'm on E."

PLASTIC LETTERS: MAY–OCTOBER 1977

Our increasing difficulties with Gary Valentine were creating an ever widening rift. He was going to leave the band right after we got back from England, but the situation dragged on. When I brought "Denis Denis" into rehearsal and suggested we try it out he didn't want to do it. Chris liked it, so did Clem, and Jimmy thought it was okay, but every time I tried to get him to do it Gary thought it was boring and kept making fun of me. I got real keyed up about this and said, "Look, it's a pretty song. I think if we do an oldie right the American DJs will play it, and I think we could have a hit." We were hardly getting any radio play and I thought it would put us over on the radio. Who knew it would be a No. 1 hit in England? I wasn't even thinking about foreign countries. I just wanted to break in the States.

Gary has a very strong personality and he didn't like to bend, like we all had to, to solve a problem. He's brilliant but very idealistic, and he really wanted to assert himself. This rivalry was going back and forth and driving us wacko. Clem was close to him because they'd been to high school together, but the problem was still there for the rest of us. Finally we couldn't get along about anything. Leeds stepped in and made the final decision, seeing the continuing dissension was having a negative effect, and he thought we were being wishy-washy. He called Gary up and said, "You're fired," which was callous because Gary had wanted to play on the second record and felt ripped off. However, he couldn't handle what was going on, so the breakup was really a mutual decision and, although we did a great song by him ("I'm always touched by your) Presence, Dear," which was his legacy to us and a hit in England and Europe, Gary Valentine didn't play on *Plastic Letters.*

Throughout this time we were preparing to record. In June we were booked into the studio again with Richard Gottehrer producing. We wanted to keep working with him because we thought he was good. We were also signed to him and didn't have any other alternative. We had so many songs among us we considered making a double album, but were discouraged by our faltering relationship with Private Stock, who were proving hopeless at marketing our product. We

The kitchen in the 17th Street apartment before the fire.

hired Frank "The Freak" Infante, another friend of Clem's, to play bass. When we went back into Plaza Sound everything was traumatic. Clem was unhappy about Gary's leaving. We didn't know if Frankie was going to be in the band. We wanted to get the album done and we had the songs, so even though we didn't have all the players, we went into the studio and made the record. Gottehrer was still taking vacations. During the six scattered weeks we spent recording *Plastic Letters* he must have been away for at least two, which makes him a miracle worker as well as a great producer.

By the time we made *Plastic Letters* there was a major difference. We wanted to be accepted for what we were. We wanted the album to emphasize high voltage rock and sound more like we did. We also wanted to get away from the nostalgia peg we were being hung on. Blondie wasn't getting anything like the serious attention we deserved. Even though we were doing just as much, too much emphasis was being put on what I looked like or who I sounded like. One review started off saying my head was too big for my body. It got me mad that we were on stage selling one thing and they were buying another. Much of what we were doing was being ignored. There was nothing to do except keep writing songs that were satisfying and that's what we did. The music was always the most important thing.

Richard was listening to us more than he had on the first album so we were much more involved with the production. He was also working more carefully. Previously he didn't have a fix on what we were doing or what we were, and that nostalgia tag came from the girl group sound. The Blondie material had improved and we all automatically bounced into "our sound" with *Plastic Letters*.

Halfway through making the record Peter Leeds came into the studio and said, "I hate Private Stock Records and we're getting off." We looked up to him enough to think, "He's up, he's Mr. Energetic College Boy, like Kennedy in his sneakers and preppy shirts." So we said, "Great! Go for it! Kill them!" And got back to making our music. Two weeks later on Labor Day weekend the whole band, excluding Gary, found themselves in a lawyer's office in a midnight contract-signing session with Chrysalis before we'd even finalized our separation from Private Stock, for which Chrysalis (i.e., ultimately us) put up $500,000. These lawyers kept us there all night while they had their discussions. Lawyers love to sit up all night in their shirtsleeves in smoke-filled rooms screaming at each other in between running to the bathroom to take aspirins. They don't even get high or drink in order to do all this.

Near dawn, bored out of our minds, we dashed over to Central Park, copped some joints, came back, and

Devo in Devo.

Back in L.A.

proceeded to get fucked up and demolish the lawyer's office. We made long phone calls to Hawaii, then threw his phones out the window, took all his papers out of his desk, and wrecked the furniture. When he came in around nine A.M. we were sitting there bleary-eyed in his wrecked office and he was so horrified he couldn't even speak. He had never been so offended in his life. We signed those contracts much against Clem's wishes. He was nervous, moaning and groaning through the whole thing, tearing his hair out, and saying we were being hoodwinked. In a way he was right, but we told him he was wrong. Then we went back into the studio to finish *Plastic Letters*.

Producing something commercial is probably one of the easiest things to do. Producing something that's exciting to you and that turns out to be exciting to other people and commercial too is the hard part. I like *Plastic Letters*. It's a good album. The sound is a little weird without Gary and there was some schizophrenia going around, which I suppose is in it, but I don't think that necessarily means it's bad. *Plastic Letters* has a dark quality to it. However, we now had a positive commitment from Chrysalis, a much bigger company with better distribution than Private Stock, and they were hot to promote and develop Blondie. We were already beginning to get better press and we all thought we were great and *Plastic Letters* was the best.

The original *Plastic Letters* cover was shot at the Tropicana. Chrysalis thought it was too punkish, because I was wearing a pillowcase with red tape striped around it and the boys had on leather, so we had to re-shoot in New York. We rented a police car for some shots in the street and coincidentally a sign in the store across the street captured in the photograph read *Plastic Letters*. Terry Ellis, the president of Chrysalis, suggested we use that as the title.

As soon as the record was finished Leeds insisted we go and play the Whiskey in L.A. for six nights so Chrysalis, which is based there, could see what it had bought. We did this against our better judgment because we didn't have the band together and we needed time to regroup. But the pace was beginning to pick up now and things were getting so frantic that we didn't have much choice but to go. Soon we were moving too fast to maintain control of what was happening around us and we had to leave it all up to Peter. He would say, "Oh I signed a contract and you have to play here." Or, "The record company expects you to go there and do some promo." The L.A. shows were pretty bad. Frankie couldn't really play bass so he played bass on half the songs and Chris played on the others. John Cassavetes and Sam Shaw filmed these shows for a projected movie called Blondie, which never happened.

We had a good time staying at the Tropicana. We

Divine.

liked the climate and the punk kids in L.A. Then we came back to New York and played CBGB's, where we broke the house record previously set by The Ramones and they had to call the fire department. Then we went back to L.A. for a second series of West Coast gigs and started setting up the world tour. "In the Flesh," the single off our first album, was climbing the Australian charts and we'd been invited to play there. We couldn't help being excited about actually having a hit record, something was happening, look out world.

Nigel Harrison, who'd seen us on the Iggy tour, came to one of our L.A. shows. We liked him and went to see him playing in Ray Manzarek's group Nite City. We asked him to come down to the Whiskey to play with us at a sound check. We didn't know that Nigel had taped our show the previous night and learned all the songs before he came to the audition, so we thought, "Hey, this guy learns quick!" and began to think about asking him to join the group on bass. Terry Ellis thought Mike Chapman should produce our next record. He liked us and was still interested, so we visited him in the studio where he was recording Suzie Quatro, and talked about it some more.

In San Francisco we got a call from Chris's mother in the middle of the night saying our apartment had burned down. This news did nothing for our nerves.

We were freaked out, particularly since she didn't know the extent of the damage, but then she called back and said that the cats were safe and that Jimmy's sister, who was staying at the apartment, luckily wasn't there that night, so she hadn't gotten burned to a crisp and the damage wasn't that bad. An electrical fire had started in what once was the kitchen, but most of our stuff was okay, although we of course now had no place to live. We always thought it was Mr. Brown's maniac who started it.

An actress named Maria Duval was our downstairs neighbor on 17th Street. When the fire began her dogs smelled the smoke and woke her in time to escape. Chris took the photo of me in the charred remains of Marilyn Monroe's original dress from *The Seven Year Itch,* bought at auction by Maria. The dress was burned beyond repair, but at least there was enough of it left for these shots. Among other things destroyed Chris lost his entire collection of *Fly* comics. He'd collected them because there were so few it was easy to get the whole set. Simultaneously the single "Denis Denis" was released in Europe and the U.K.

The landlord had reassured us over the phone while we were still in California that everything would be all cleaned up for us when we came back. He was apologetic about the fire and said we would be able to move back in, but when we got there every-

Car culture.

The famous Camaro.

Rob Freeman and Richard Gottehrer working on Plastic Letters *at* Plaza Sound.

Recording the footsteps on Denis Denis.

Debbie with Alan and Marty Suicide.

Thunders, Sable Starr, Walter Lure, Jeffrey Salen.

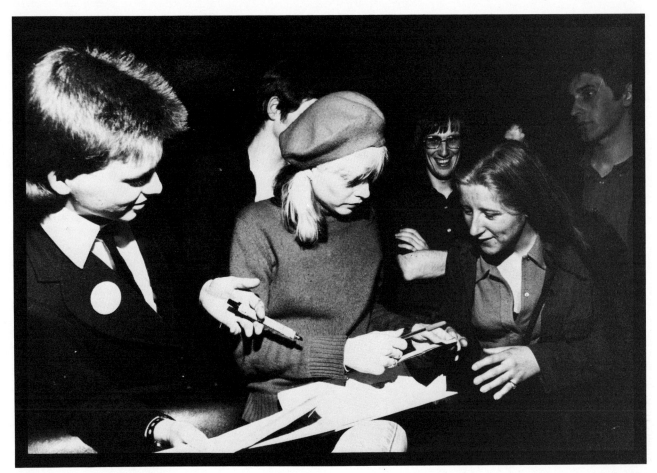

Debbie signs autographs, Glasgow.

thing had been shoveled into a pile of burned rubble in the kitchen. The only thing that had been cleaned out was my jewelry box, which contained my gold charm bracelet. So, while the cats stayed hidden in the farthest corner of the bedroom closet, still traumatized from being nearly barbecued, we dug through the remains, put everything that was worth saving covered with soot in sooty boxes, and stuffed them in storage. We checked into the Gramercy Park Hotel for three days, found a temporary home for the three cats with my sister, and packed for the world tour.

Leeds had given out the world tour schedule, which was Terry Ellis's plan to make us internationally known. The first step was my trip to Australia with Leeds for a two-week publicity tour, while the rest of the band rehearsed for the U.K. November tour, which was step number two of the master plan.

We were each given $500 by the record company to buy clothes. Most of my money went on shoes because that's one thing you can't get in the garbage or drug stores. Then I left for Australia with Leeds.

While I was gone Chris moved into the Edison, a hotel near Times Square, that had eleven thousand identical, tiny rooms covered with thick layers of pink paint. Frankie and Nigel were hired on for the tour before I left town, and Nigel only had twenty-

four hours to pack and get to the city for ten days of crammed-in rehearsals. He came to New York the next day and moved into a pink room opposite Chris's at the Edison so he could learn all the material. Chris kept Sunday Man with him in the little room, but the maid, who had a deep scar on her face, wouldn't come into the room because she was terrified of cats.

THE WORLD TOUR:
OCTOBER 1977– FEBRUARY 1978

On October 24, 1977, I was in Melbourne squinting under the harsh glare of some TV studio lights. My day had begun in New York and had included a round of TV, radio, and magazine interviews in New Zealand. Every time I stepped off a plane I was flying with the sun, effectively cramming two days' work into one, but on the set of Channel 7's "Nightmoves" my day was slowly coming to a close. I had on a short black dress, a long black leather coat, thigh high black leather boots, and black tights. All the reporter wanted to know was whether I ripped my dress off on stage during "Rip Her To Shreds." I tried to explain that it was theatrical ripping, not stripping. However, the Australian press seemed riveted by this image of me ripping my clothes off and singing stark naked, and wouldn't stop asking me about it.

Just before he left for England November 1 to meet us there, Chris called me in Melbourne at The Southern Cross Hotel. It was three o'clock in the afternoon in New York, but it was three o'clock in the morning in Melbourne so he woke me up, and all I was able to tell him about Australia at that time was that the water goes counterclockwise down the drain rather than clockwise. When Chris left New York to go on the world tour, Sunday Man went to my sister's house too.

On November 2 Leeds and I flew from Sydney to London where we joined Chris at the Montcalm Hotel in London's West End.

The visit to Australia had been worthwhile in that it gave me the opportunity to get a perspective on what Peter Leeds was up to and what he thought he "had" in me. I was tired of Leeds pushing me around. He was totally disrespectful, and by the time I arrived in London I'd had it with him. Chris and I stayed at the Montcalm for a couple of days. We were really happy to see each other and be alone together but we were both exhausted.

When the rest of the band flew in on November 5, we moved into a cheaper room at the Royal Gardens Hotel on Kensington High Street, while Leeds and our publicist Famous Toby Mamis stayed on at the Montcalm. "Denis Denis," which was our first English No. 1 hit, was being used as a football song in stadiums across England and Scotland. We got pretty friendly with The Damned, Sue Cat Woman, a journalist named Chris Needs, and Lemme from Motorhead. Clem became particularly friendly with The Jam.

Most of the time we were working hard, rehearsing, doing TV shows, performing, or doing interviews. I was working constantly. The only people who got to go out were the guys in the band because they didn't have to do as much press as I did. I was working all the time, and clubbing wasn't that much fun knowing you had to get up early for a photo session. But I saw some other bands, plus ran into some New Yorkers. Nancy Spungeon, whom I'd gotten to know very well in New York, had moved to London, and Johnny Thunders and The Heartbreakers were getting up there and recording, under Lee Childers's cool hand as their manager then. Jerry Nolan was on drums. Also, apart from The Ramones, Talking Heads, and Wayne County, The Dictators were on tour. Siouxsie and the Banshees were starting to get good notices, and Poly Styrene was terrific. The Pistols, The Clash, and The Stranglers were also playing on home ground.

On this second tour of England we were headlining to an enthusiastic clique audience in the larger clubs and small halls that we should have played on the first tour. Only this time we were much more popular and would play halls with 1,500 people and have to turn away 700. This was phenomenal for us. Leeds was flipping out, screaming, "Oh my God, why are they booking us into these small halls." Here we were

playing in clubs that hold 200 people and turning away 500, which actually happened in one place. (Unfortunately one of the 500 turned out to be from Led Zeppelin, we learned later.) The places would get so hot that the walls perspired and everything was hung with moisture. This was at the height of the spitting period when everybody spit at you if you were good. You had to hold back because if you jumped around too much and got too enthused they'd spit at you. Sometimes it was fun and good-natured but sometimes they would just do it to be obnoxious. There's a difference between friendly and unfriendly spit. Once Chris started banging this guy on the head with his guitar because he was spitting at him and everybody was going "yaa yaa." The guy pulled the guitar away from Chris so he jumped into the audience after it. Then somebody else grabbed the guitar and was making off through the crowd with it, but Chris and Michael Sticca followed the cord. Everybody kept playing until they turned the lights up, then everybody stopped. They got the guitar back and Chris still has it today, but he lost the cord. I like that funky intimate excitement of clubs the best.

Things with Leeds were not going very well, however, and when Chris complained that he was treating us like children Leeds screamed and threw him out of his hotel room a couple of times, which was a bad mistake.

When we returned to London we played the Rainbow. It was a weird gig because the press was criticizing me for being too sexy. At that point I was still reading the papers so I decided I would just stand still for the Rainbow gig. The next day the press said, "She didn't move around at all! She just stood there!" After that I chose to ignore their comments.

After playing the Rainbow in London, we played Paris, Amsterdam, and Munich. Then Leeds and Mamis returned to the States while we continued on, via London, to Australia.

AUSTRALIA

The British Airways flight stopped in Bahrain. We didn't get out of the plane because it was a short twenty-minute stop, but we stuck our heads out and sniffed the air. It smelled African, and in the distance we saw a magical-looking lit pavillion. A number of old men in turbans, who looked as if they should have been pashas in Rangoon, got on the plane to clean. There were far too many of them employed to do the job and they were skinny, and looked uptight. They frowned at us intensely and obviously hated us. They must have gotten ten cents each for their work.

These thirty-six-hour flights from England to Australia are always packed to the gunwales with silver-haired grandmothers, retired men going to Australia to relax, and children en route to visit grandparents who've already retired to the sunshine. We were jammed in like cattle, packed like sardines. Every seat in economy class was taken, so we couldn't

Clem and Jimmy enplane, Singapore Airport.

stretch out. Chris and I had a spitting baby in front of us. At one point Chris was in a dazed sort of sleep and all of a sudden this brat spat up PHFFFFFT! right in his face. Chris smacked it with a pillow and the mother leaped up horrified, thinking that Chris was a bona fide child molestor who was actually going to pillow her little spitter. We sure were attracting our share of spit in those days. Our next stop was Singapore, where we did manage to get out of the plane for twenty minutes.

Finally, after this grueling flight, we landed on the west coast of Australia in Perth, to be greeted by a bunch of athletic Australians in white shorts and hats, who rushed into the plane and sprayed the whole cabin with bug spray before anyone could move. After thrity-six hours scrunched up, wheezed at, spat on, and finally sprayed with DDT, we deplaned in Perth.

Record executives and promoters met us at the airport and escorted us into town. It was a hot, beautiful heady night with a full moon and there was a gorgeous blooming smell. When we got to the hotel we found out John Denver was staying there, too. In fact, he was to dog our steps throughout the tour. It is accepted that you have to recover from the flight to Australia. Businessmen aren't allowed to work for two days after they get there for fear their judgment may be impaired. However, we had a sound check at eleven the next morning, because we were playing that night.

We had no end of problems getting our sound and lights halfway decent. Our Australian tour manager Ray McGuire looked like Rod Stewart but at the time stuttered like a maniac. The show was to be in the Perth Concert Hall, which was brand new but looked as if it had been built in the nineteenth century and had an air of antiseptic sterility. Perth is a bastion of Christian conservatism. The audience had no idea what we were like because all they'd heard was "In the Flesh," which is a conventional pretty ballad, so all the moms and dads had come with their kids. We even got a bouquet of flowers onstage from the Mayor of Perth, who was probably disgusted when he saw our act. They must have all thought we were terrible. Apart from their not knowing anything about New Wave music, we were extremely uncoordinated after this twelve-hour time change. Everybody was totally zonked, since in effect we were doing the gig at eight in the morning. I made a kick-jump and couldn't control my legs, landed in a split, and couldn't get back up. During the finale Frankie threw his guitar up in the air and stood there as it crashed onto the stage and broke into little pieces. We liked this concert because it was definitely hallucinogenic.

After the gig everybody flipped out. Ray McGuire started smashing beer cans on his head and told us

Australian hotel life.

Objects floating in swimming pool after night of Australian hotel life. Note Adelaide 1977-1978 Telephone Directory.

how Uri Geller had just been through the previous week and levitated the building. Everybody was very impressed by this and insisted they'd seen him do it. Ray kept on smashing beer cans on his head. Then he said we should go to Beethoven's, the Studio 54 of Perth, but when we got there they wouldn't let us in because we were wearing T-shirts and sneakers. When they were finally persuaded to make an exception in our case, we rushed into what looked like the dining room of a Howard Johnson motel. We got drunk as quickly as we could and went to a pizza parlor jammed with people, where Clem and Jimmy started a food fight. All of a sudden Jimmy jumped up and started chasing Clem, as if he were going to kill him. Clem started turning tables and chairs over behind him as he ran, and the five pizza makers vaulted over the counter and jumped on both of them in order to avoid the massive brawl they imagined was about to break out. The pizza men, complete with aprons and chef's hats, held Jimmy and Clem down. Everybody was horrified. And the record executives, who thought we were lunatic funky idiot savages, quickly took us back to the hotel, where we smoked a little pot and talked to our opening band, The Ferrets, who claimed they saw UFO's constantly. The Ferrets had formed nineteen months previously and had had a No. 1 hit single with their second record, "Don't Fall In Love." However, the band, five guys and two very pretty sisters, had an image so incongruous with what they did that they were always at odds with themselves. They couldn't suddenly put on black leather pants and change their whole image. They played Lou Reed music and wore hippie clothes. We liked them and got along well together. As far as drugs were concerned it was pretty hard to get any pot in Australia, which was sort of weird because we heard there was a lot of smack coming down from Asia. The dumb thing was people were ODing like crazy on the Gold Coast, but while we were there the authorities appeared to be busting people who had two pot plants in their backyards. The next day we flew to Adelaide and talked to the press.

"In The Flesh" was No. 2 on the charts, but they still didn't know what New Wave was so they probably thought we were just a crummy band who couldn't play properly. After playing Adelaide we went on to Melbourne where I saw a couple of Aborigines in the street. I was surprised at how tall they are. I didn't see any small ones. We also met David Gulpilil, the star of *Walkabout* and *The Last Wave,* at the screening of *Wave* in Melbourne. He was vibrant and sweet. That's also where we played a great gig on December 1, at a fun fair down by the beach called the Palais Theatre. It was a big occasion, the kids were wild and enthusiastic. They

Debbie at Sydney harbor.

applauded like crazy, swarmed around the dressing room, and afterwards didn't want to let us leave.

Everybody was surprised by how young they were, thinking we were going to have a much older audience. When they realized how upbeat we were, the critics, promoters, and church people got nervous, and I was held up as a bad example. They always exaggerated what I did, still maintaining, for example, that I tore my clothes off when I sang "Rip Her To Shreds." Everywhere I went that was the first question I was asked: "Uh, yes, we hear that you, uh, TEAR YOUR CLOTHES OFF IN PERFORMANCE? AAAHHHH!" That was all they wanted to know about, proving further that sex is the universal language.

In the beginning of the tour we were highly enthusiastic. We were a national group. Everywhere we went people hit on us for autographs, there were lookalike contests, and lots of bands were forming. We were obviously controversial and they wanted me to be a rude wild girl to fit the information about our being a punk group; also I wore leather, whereas ankle-length flowered skirts were in style. They looked like sixties hippies not sixties mods, and the older people were definitely living in the fifties. The hip kids had caught onto New Wave fashion, but were a pitiful minority back then.

By the time we got back to Melbourne to play the Palais Theatre again, everybody was tired and burned out. We were walking through the airport fighting and bitching at each other when we got shoved into a waiting room for a press conference. Everybody was cursing each other, threatening to punch each other out, screaming "I'll kick your ass!" in front of the press people, who thought this was truly bad, and the next day they had a picture of me in the papers looking mean, with dark glasses and a little skull and crossbones on my leather jacket. The caption read: *New York's five-man and one-woman punk rock group Blondie hit Melbourne yesterday—and it took less than a minute for the swearing, belching and rude antagonism to begin. Even the group's promoters, Evans Gudinski and Associates, walked out of a press interview. Lead singer Deborah Harry said she wasn't sure Australia was "ready for us yet." Her use of four letter words belied her press release description which said she was "actress, personality, a human being with depth, sensitivity . . ."* One day as we were walking in the street a pissed-off extremely affected guy came hurtling past and yelled, "Why don't you go back to America where you are somebody?" What a sense of humor.

Basically, the kids loved us. Lou Reed had just been through Australia and had played two-hour sets with his back to the audience. All the pretty girls in the cities were very happy to tell us they were mov-

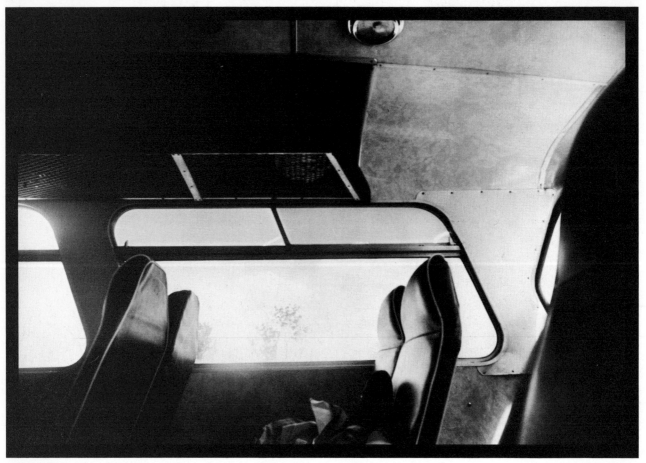

Australian tour bus.

ing to New York or London. Inside Australia there was a whole other network of people in little towns who told us they were all moving to the big cities. At least there were a lot of pretty girls for the guys to go crazy over, except they all had boyfriends when we got out into the smaller towns. We worked in some small towns bordering the outback that were one street thirteen hours from nowhere. We'd spend the entire day traveling across the semi-desert in the bus and by the time we arrived it would be caked with piss, dirt, sweat, grime, and shit. Jimmy was constantly smashing his keyboards and saying he wanted to go home. Our entire crew of two broke their asses doing what they had to do. Naturally we felt obligated to maintain a genuine rock'nroll attitude. Consequently, there was a lot of hotel room trashing.

The Ferrets had a football and whenever the bus had to stop for repairs they would jump out and start kicking the football around. One time one of the sisters kicked their football too hard and sprained her ankle. So she had to do the rest of the tour with a cast on her foot sitting down on the stage or on crutches. We never knew what happened to The Ferrets after our tour.

During a long ride on the bus Ray told us the story of how he came to stutter. He was tooling along on his motorcycle at a hundred miles an hour in the desert, when he unexpectedly crashed head-on into a herd of wild horses. He woke up embedded in this horse's breast with his motorcycle, and both of his arms and legs broken. The horse was still moaning and twitching. Ever since the accident Ray had his stutter. I think he was the same guy on that tour who once bit off a big roach's head and washed it down with piss saying, "MMMMmmm, good piss this." If my memory is correct, it seems the ghost of Eduardo haunted us briefly in Australia. We kept looking for more Aborigines, but were told that they were drunk in the woods, and we didn't want to talk to them. The way the Aborigines are treated makes our treatment of the Indians look positively noble.

I noticed a quite beautiful mauve-violet-purple-fuchsia color everywhere in Australia. They also have cars that color purple and, by odd coincidence, they made up big purple Blondie buttons so all the Blondie promo material was also that color. I've never seen it anywhere else. There's one famous tree that blossoms with these beautiful colors, and because of the angle of the earth, when the sun sets, the sky erupts in a purple storm every single night, which to me was perfection because when I was in high school the walls and ceilings of my room were that color purple—violet.

The schedule we had was much more relaxed than our English one, but they kept us pretty busy. In between shows we did a lot of press, TV, and radio,

Debbie and Anya Phillips, hotel room, Baltimore.

Punk Boutique (BOY), Kings Road, London.

Kim Fowley.

Eddie Dugan and friend.

102

Richard Hell poolside at the Tropicana, L.A.

Debbie on the river, Bangkok.

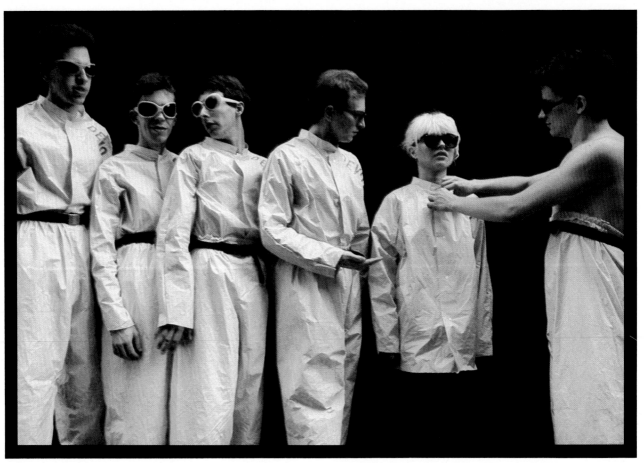

Debbie Devolves.

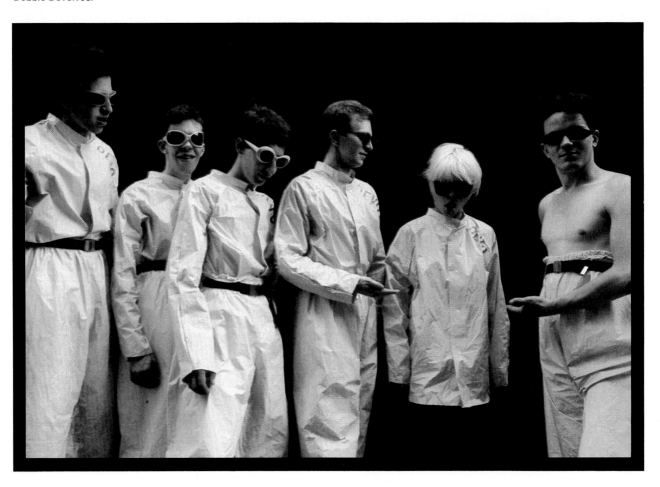

Australian T.V. announcer wearing Debbie Harry T-shirt.

and went to the beach, or met other musicians and went shopping. They have souvenirs on sale like kangaroo heads and/or one hoof sticking out of a piece of wheel. When I travel through different landscapes the strangeness of it makes me feel that I'm not there and other times I think that I've changed size. I felt much taller in Australia than, say, in Florida, and I feel bigger in New York than in Florida, but I think I'm smaller when I'm in France or England. I think somehow or other I change sizes in other areas, but my clothes still fit everywhere I go so forget it.

Wednesday, December 21, to Friday, December 28, we were booked to have a vacation on Keppel Island, which is a semi-tropical isle in the Great Barrier Reef, where we were to do three concerts in exchange for room and board. This was a straight resort for families, a bit like an English holiday camp. There were a few young people there, but it was mostly adults.

On Christmas day, Clem, Frankie, and Chris decided they would go on a boatride to one of the surrounding islands. On the way the waves pushed their boat up against some sharp coral reefs which cut up the bottom. The boat started to sink, the engine fell off, and the boys had to scramble onto a little island where equally sharp coral cut up their feet. They were late coming back, and fearing they had been eaten by sharks I sent out the old salt whose job it was to rescue drowning vacationers, and he found them huddled on this reef. The old salt told them there was nothing worse than cunts at sea, towed the boat back, and made them pay for it and the motor. At least they managed to make the gig that night. We jammed and played bar music three nights in a row for the twenty-five or thirty people who happened to be hanging out.

The high point of this visit came when some thieves came to the island and robbed everybody. They checked out people's habits and hit the rooms when everyone was out. They stole a watch from us and $300 in cash, which was our savings. We discovered our losses late at night. I was furious and started screaming, "I hate this place!"—trying to wake everyone up. Everybody else discovered they had had something taken and there was a general outcry.

The thieves made good their escape on the following morning, but we had seen them lurking around the day before, so when the Townsville Chief of Police arrived to question everybody, we were able to give a vague description of what they looked like. The police apprehended them, and dragged them in chains back to the mainland where they were led off to spend the next hundred years in jail. Everybody was muttering about the terrible fate that awaited them. We were glad to fly back to Sydney on December 28, from where we took a nine-thirty P.M. flight to

105

Stuffed snake, Ambassador hotel, Bangkok.

Bangkok, Thailand. We had been booked to do four gigs in Thailand over the New Year while we waited for our Japanese dates, which weren't until the middle of January. Our last look at Australia was over beautiful Sydney and the harbor.

THAILAND

We arrived in Bangkok airport around six A.M. Some young airport officials, half of them wearing uniforms and the other half in plainclothes, stood around in dark glasses smoking cigarettes, and there were two gorgeous Thai girls, also waiting. The whole scene looked like a sleazy "B" movie. We were immediately intrigued. The promoter of our concerts, a Mr. Idibah, also the Chief of Police and owner of numerous radio stations that were playing our album, came to meet us with his tall skinny assistant, who was constantly rubbing his hands together. They were both courteous professionals, but on our arrival everything seemed like a caricature and luckily the gorgeous girls turned out to be fans.

It was just getting light as we drove into Bangkok. Everybody was pouring into the streets. The roads were starting to fill up with people marching back and forth with bags on their backs, carrying out their daily chores. By the time we got into the city the entire landscape was moving. Campfires burned everywhere. We immediately got a sense of a completely different sea of humanity. It was outlawville.

The Ambassador Hotel was super modern and full of international intrigue with German, Japanese, and English tourists stylishly smoking their cigarettes. We walked right into a Hitchcock movie. We went up to our rooms, which were fine except for the pillows, which were so hard you couldn't possibly put your head on them. They were packed with wood shavings. Maybe they were for opium smokers. Eventually we figured you could call down for regular pillows. Anyway, we passed out for a while, then got up and began to wander around the city seeing the sights. We were immediately digging on how densely mystical the whole place was.

If you went out the motorized glass door of our deluxe hotel and turned left, one block away the paved street turned to dirt and there was a vile little river of a sewer full of stinking waste covered with a white film of scum. We expected to see a head float by any minute. It smelled like death. Two blocks away we bumped into lepers with no fingers. We'd been used to seeing the bums in New York, who look at you with expressions of horror that are mostly put-ons. When these guys looked at us with expres-

On the river, Bangkok.

sions of horror, it was because their arms ended in red stumps.

We went down to the river and visited the snake farms where they keep all sorts of different precious animals jammed into cages so tourists can come and ogle them. There was a huge pit full of twenty hissing cobras next to a pit of mongooses, which are the cobra's polar opposite and eternal enemy. When we came in, the caretaker asked us if we wanted to see them fight. We said, "No, no, no," but he pulled out a giant cobra and threw it on the ground in front of me and it started hissing. He poked it around and then threw it back into the pit. While all this was going on some little children at a commune day school were chanting a political song off in the distance and music from a tiny loudspeaker was wafting through.

We also visited the ancient walled city. It's a large area of traditional old buildings that's heavily fortified and has armed security men with guns and mortars, protecting all their old icons from terrorists or international thieves. That was, however, the only sign of soldiers we saw. Everywhere else in Bangkok all we saw was an occasional traffic cop. It was pretty peaceful.

The river, which runs through the centre of the city, is the source of life. People wash their clothes in it, use it for cooking water, and as a communal sewer. They also swim in it. It flows so fast it washes every-

thing away with it. Whole families, with all their possessions, live in small shacks on stilts sticking out of the water. They have no walls, just a platform and roof with pieces of cloth hanging down. It's overgrown and primitive. They also have long gondolas with regular V-8 car engines mounted on the back. Instead of a drive shaft there's a long propellor on a pole, and they paint the boats.

Bangkok is one of the great classic cities of the world where you can see a typical clash of the modern and the traditional, but the assimilation of the modern is happening with breathtaking speed. We did four shows at the Ambassador Hotel on New Year's Eve and New Year's Day. They had the ballroom set up for us and they had a beautiful brand new PA system.

Bangkok is one of two places in the world where the electricity is not grounded. When the electricity is going through all the offices during the day, industry uses it up so it keeps going around. But when all the industry switches off at night, gobs of electricity are left floating around with nowhere to go, and may come bursting out anywhere, anytime. Nobody in Bangkok is an electronics expert, to say the least, but this brand new concert-size PA system was to be quite a challenge to set up. From a technical point of view the way they put the gig together was as much of a show as we were: it was a devotional act.

Thai Temple.

Debbie and friend.

Miniature Thai Temple.

109

Cobra pit.

At the most you need ten people to put up sound and lights, but I swear there were maybe fifty guys crawling over, under and around mountains of wires, one of whom knew what he was doing, sort of. We never thought they were going to get it together. They'd have a whole Medusa's head of wires, none of which were numbered or labeled, so that if one fucked up they'd have to unplug everything and start all over again. We saw guys praying to wires. It should take about three or four hours, but it took three days for these fifty guys to put up the PA. Meanwhile it was a cool hundred degrees the whole time. They made Blondie cutouts, logos, and styrofoam lettering nicely painted with glitter, but then, as soon as the first crowd showed up—zoom—everything was gone. No one minded, though; the clever Thais produce millions of different artifacts and make a lot of instant art. There are so many people to employ you can get anything you want done in Thailand: for $5 a hundred people will come over and paint your house in twenty seconds. And they can copy anything.

Our New Year's Eve concerts were billed as The First Punk Rock concerts in Asia, and they were a fascinating success. The audiences, an invigorating mixture of Brits, Aussies, Yanks, Japs, sailors, nurses, moms, dads, kids and students, looked at us and we at them. By far the most colorful was an Indian man in a turban accompanying seven women in saris holding their babies in their arms.

Because the electricity wasn't grounded, power surges occurred during all four shows. While we were playing everything peaked awesomely, all of a sudden quadrupling in volume for five seconds. Beer bottles jumped off the amps. Fortunately the audience thought it was part of the show. Blondie's shows were over by nine P.M. on New Year's Eve so the hotel invited us to dinner as their guests at the rooftop restaurant.

They threw this lavish party on the roof of the hotel which was all hooplahed up for New Year's Eve. It was as decadent as they could possibly make it. All these rich Europeans were looking at row upon row of wasted food and ice sculptures while the lepers wallowed in the sewers a block away. They wanted us to play at the party but somehow we managed to get out of that. So we sat there getting drunk and began to freak out.

After dinner we were invited to a young Thai journalist's house. At the midnight hour we were crunched in a mini enroute to Patpong, and everybody leaned out of their little open vehicles and started yelling and screaming and careening around; this was the appropriate place to be since you weren't allowed to be on the streets after midnight.

In Patpong, the nightclub section, the bar girls

More temple.

have numbers. They seemed to know certain men as regulars, and they made a fuss over the guys in the band. I think they were happy to see some westerners; naturally business died down after the war was over. They really know their business inside out. It's an acknowledged profession to be a bar girl and to dance, seduce men, and earn favors. Only the most beautiful girls get to do it. These girls were sophisticated and naive, experienced and innocent. They didn't speak terrific English, but they got along fine. They were measuring to see which one of the guys had the biggest cock and they were all giggling and voting for one of the guys, saying, "Oh yes!" Nigel was making out with one girl at the table, but none of the guys picked any of the girls up, although some of them were unbelievably beautiful. There'd always be one in each bar who looked like a model.

Patpong has great funky tinky honky tonk neon lights. There were also a lot of expatriates there. One man claimed to have been in Sounds Incorporated, a five-piece instrumental band that opened up for the Beatles on their first American tour. While we were doing the concerts we were on the radio a lot and some of the girls were dancing to our songs in the bars. Because of the ungrounded electricity, anybody who can put up an aerial in Bangkok can open a radio station. There are no regulations whatsoever. Whoever gets the more powerful signal gets the air-

waves. When you tune the dial there are constant stations.

Patpong is like a G.I. Joe stateside fantasy of Sin City. It's wide open, you can get anything you want in this very sensuous atmosphere and climate. Patpong glowed all night in funky neon splendor. The painted boats zoomed around the river, the people burned incense in front of golden statues, the dancers danced, the lovers loved, we felt like history.

When we were there, for $18 you could get a pair of custom tailored jeans on Sukhumvit Road that fit tighter than your $40 Fioruccis, a Thai silk shirt made to your specifications went for $12. All was not paradise though. Apart from the lepers and sewers, the traffic jams were worse than in New York rush hours and a walk on a busy street could be overwhelmingly hot and smelly. But the children are beautiful; they sell flowers in the street and smile and laugh at the drop of a hat. We alternately heard that Thailand was run by the Red Chinese and the C.I.A. Being fairly apolitical I couldn't care less, but Bangkok was returning to the people after a long time and it was a quiet revolution like nothing I'd felt before.

The most interesting experiences Chris and I had were some psychic communications. One night we were both semi-asleep in two separate beds. Chris was floating in an astral state, thinking, "Where are we? We must be in bed," when I said out loud, "Yes, I

Nigel and Debbie, Tokyo.

think so." I was also ill for a few days and had a series of astral projections, dreams, and psychic sexual experiences. The Thais language is so musical and soft. Of all the Asian people, they say that the Thais are the most sensuous. They're very friendly warm people. Everybody was so helpful, after a few days we didn't even need guides.

JAPAN

After ten glorious days in Bangkok we flew to Tokyo. Everybody told us the Japanese customs were murder, but the customs man didn't bother to look through our bags at all. Peter Leeds, who wanted to take the opportunity to see Japan, joined us in Tokyo. I could definitely live there. It's so civilized, respectful, clean, and science-fiction pretty. Bright red, yellow, and blue sci-fi robot neon colors are everywhere. The Japanese food is mostly protein, there are no down type of drugs, except alcohol, and there isn't any pot in Japan. Considering the hours we'd been keeping, everybody felt energized and we became insomniacs. There was no way to fall asleep and do the shows every day, so the whole band lay awake for two weeks. We were booked into one of the

great hotels in Tokyo, but the second night we were there Chris and I were lying in our room trying to catch five minutes of sleep when all of a sudden we heard Frankie and Sticca running in the halls screaming, "The yellow peril! The yellow peril!" Next thing, crash bash they took one of those neat Japanese pictures off the wall and pitched it out into the hall where it smashed into a million pieces. They rushed out, dragged the pieces back into the room and hid them under the bed, but naturally first thing in the morning the maid discovered them. Everyone was horrified, and we got thrown out of the hotel immediately. We had to move to a lower-class part of town. We thought it was funny. Leeds was pissed off.

The Japanese have a very strong moral code. They work for Japan. The only problem is, they don't know the meaning of the word "No." They said "Yes. Now we are going to so and so for gigantic wonderful press conference with one hundred photographers and two thousand reporters that you must speak to for the next two days." I said, "No, I don't think I can do this."

"Okay, no," they said. "Now we go to wonderful luncheon with press photographers and reporters that you can speak to."

I said, "No, no. I'm not going."

"Oh yes. Okay," they said, "Now we can go have your picture taken for much magazine."

Backstage, Tokyo.

Japanese kids playing.

Japanese women.

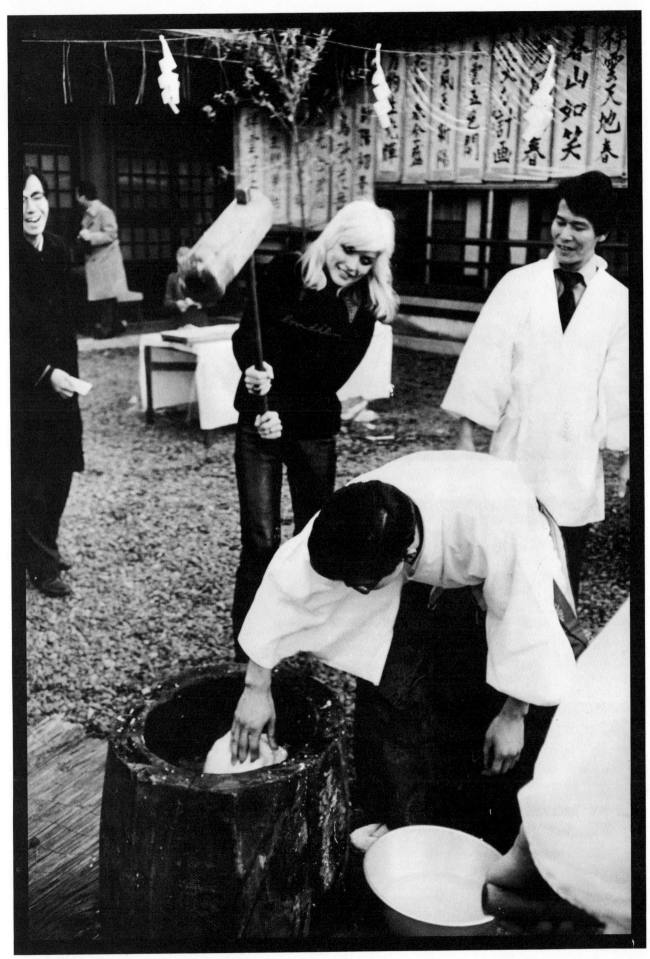

Debbie in the famous finger smashing ceremony.

Japanese soda machine.

Tokyo.

116

Back to Europe.

How ingenious. They just say the same thing over and over again, differently. I wondered what they would do if I didn't go. Would they imprison me? Or brainwash me? Or give me a karate chop? Or get me drunk on sake and drag me there anyway? Finally of course I went because, I mean, where else could I have gone? There were at least ten of these guys politely standing around waiting. But the questions they asked us on the radio blew me away. First they asked us to curse in English, so we said "Hell." But that didn't satisfy them.

"Damn?" "No . . . no . . . curse like Sex Pistols," they begged. We said, "Suck a dead donkey's dick."

Then they wanted to know how many times a day I fucked and did I have a climax on stage. Were they kidding or what? But the worst thing was, we weren't selling out the halls we were playing. After seeing us playing clubs that were too small in England, Leeds had convinced Mr. Udo, the promoter, to book us into a series of big halls.

Once, just before an encore, Chris didn't think he'd have time to make it to the bathroom and back onto the stage, and, being naive about Japanese customs and still under the influence of Eduardo, pissed backstage in a cup. The promoters went bananas, screaming, "Oh God. We've worked for forty years to get a gig in this theater. How can you do this? Our lives are in jeopardy." Luckily we managed to clean up the

piss before anyone connected to the theater got a glimpse of it and blacked out from sheer disgust.

We lost money at all the gigs. But we enjoyed touring Japan, very much. The fans are beautiful, and go absolutely overboard for rock'nroll. The Japanese don't mix politics and entertainment so they don't treat it too seriously, which is good. It's very straight. There was no hanging around dressing rooms or anything like that. Although they will jump around at concerts if you tell them to. They're really polite, but when we said, "Get up!" they all jumped up and started jumping around. Unfortunately, we didn't get to meet too many kids or have much contact with Japanese people because we were moving around so fast surrounded by rock businessmen. We did meet Mr. Gun, who got to meet all the rock stars, and he invited us to the Crocodile Club as his guests. His club is the most popular in Tokyo. He gave Jimmy a Samurai sword.

They really are into the sleazy gangster trip, and it's quite odd to see Japanese culture mixed with Chicago machismo. Mr. Gun had a number of heavy guys lurking about the Crocodile Club wearing American gangster suits and lifting weights in the back. Then when you walk around Shinjuku, which is the big amusement center, all these young gangsters are standing around on the street looking really cool wearing impeccable suits and pure white overcoats.

117

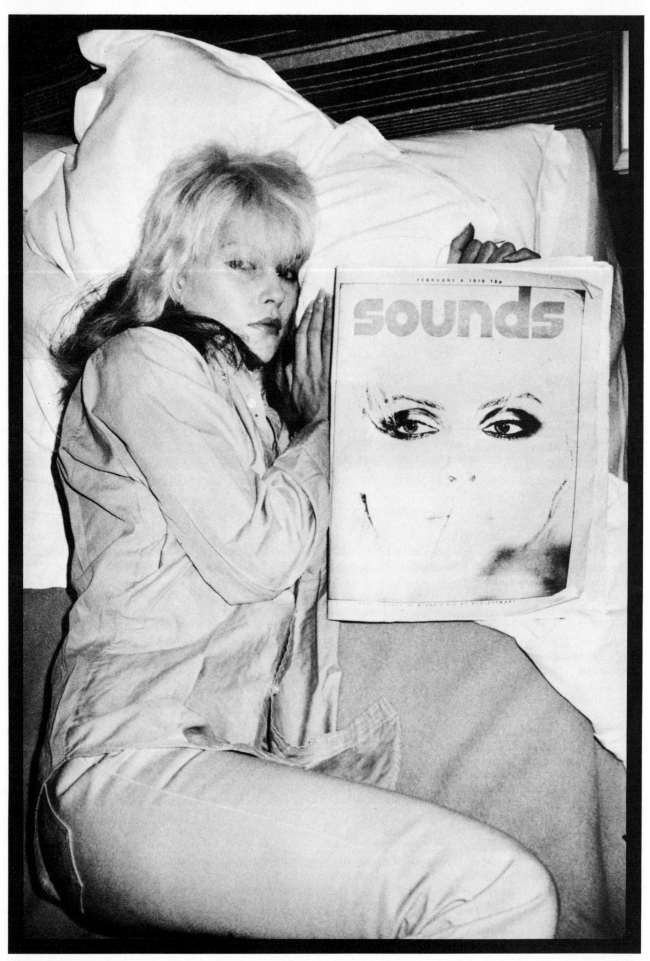

Brussels Hotel.

Cross German Express.

However, we could never figure out what kinds of weirdness they were into, because there's very little crime in Japan.

It's another world, because everything's really nice and picturesque. No matter how sleazy it is, it's always really clean. There's no dirt anywhere, and it seems as if everything excites the Japanese. They're real stimulated and like everything. It's a very positive society, but I think it makes them a little crazy.

We also went on the famous Bullet train, which goes 120 miles an hour and was supposed to get us there in twenty minutes, but it broke down and took two hours instead. "This never happened before," our guide kept saying. "It is definitely the first time this ever happened." The New Wave was only just beginning to reach Japan. It was still early and it hadn't really taken off there yet.

BACK TO EUROPE

The New Wave had taken off in Europe while we had been in Asia and Blondie was at the center of it with "Denis Denis" and "Presence Dear," both hits. So from Japan we flew straight back across Russia to London, passing over Tunguska where a UFO or meteorite crashed into Siberia in 1908. It was the biggest disaster in natural history. They saw lights in the sky in London and Paris. Our plane stopped in Moscow.

It looked like Alaska; everything covered with snow. Even the runways were white. We got out of the plane—it was freezing—and went into the terminal. People were milling around but it was quieter somehow. We must have looked pretty weird to them in our black leather jackets and sunglasses, but you're not allowed to do a doubletake in Russia, it's illegal to believe somebody else is weird, so nobody reacted. There was an enormous blond policeman patroling and tons of free literature on communism, Lenin, etc. We got a beautiful edition of the *Communist Manifesto*, which they had in eighteen different languages, and bought some Lenin souvenir badges.

We were now more exhausted and tempers were frayed on this long hop back to London. None of us had any money and we were beginning to have doubts about those contracts we had signed with Leeds back in L.A. without proper legal advice. He had power of attorney and control of all our business, and we still had to ask him for money.

On this flight he also made the boys feel more insecure than ever before by telling everyone in the group except me that he could be replaced. Imagine being in the middle of nowhere and being told you

119

Cross German Express.

can be replaced. They all went completely berserk after that. Later on, when he was even more uptight, Leeds told me I could also be replaced. We had learned a lot by error. And now, with hit singles in Europe and the second album about to come out, we were getting more and more concerned about our business future.

On January 20, 1978, we arrived in London from Tokyo. We spent a few days rehearsing and doing promo for *Plastic Letters,* which was to be released February 1. We kicked this off with a by-invitation-only gig in Dingwalls which turned out to be a disaster. Chris had a temperature of 104 from the Japanese flu and Leeds had gotten us a soundman who used to work for Kiss. Dingwalls is an acoustic nightmare. And this gig was the first we'd ever done with that soundman. We managed to stumble through most of the set with Chris leaning against an amplifier trying to look cool. However, at the end of the gig he jumped at Clem because Clem was raging away and had started the encore too fast while we were trying to tune up. Clem leaped up, turned over his drums, threw away his sticks, and dashed offstage almost knocking Jimmy over his organ. Everything went flying and everybody ran offstage chasing each other like the Marx Brothers. It was a shitty gig and we had a big duke out in the backyard of Dingwalls afterwards. The bouncers had to break it up and we

were sent back to the hotel in separate cars.

We started the European *Plastic Letters* tour at Arnhem, which is where a British paratroop invasion got the shit shot out of itself near the end of the Second World War. We felt like a rampaging army ourselves. (At this point the reader might peruse a brief history of World War II.) By the time we hit the Paradiso in Amsterdam we were playing with manic enthusiasm. We were so ragged and exhausted, but those were some of the most exciting gigs we ever did. The Paradiso is an old church converted into a club. It was jammed with people hanging off the balcony. Outside it was freezing cold but inside it was steaming hot, the walls were dripping, and everybody was throwing beer at each other. That kind of atmosphere is what enabled us to keep going even though it was the year of the red flu and we were violently ill. We practically crawled onstage on our hands and knees some nights. We had built up a momentum and we were getting a very strong response. We played Brussels and went on into France, where I wrote "Sound Asleep" which is on *Eat to the Beat.* I was going to call it "The Desperate Hours" because Chris and I were deliriously sick. They wouldn't give us any flu shots. They kept giving us anal suppositories instead. They are very big in France.

We played Lyons and Marseilles where we stayed in a motel off the Arab quarter and ran around

Cross German Express.

checking everything out for a couple of days. We kept trying to make phone calls to Marty Silfen, a young lawyer in New York we'd met previously, because we were getting even more concerned about our business involvement with Leeds, but everyone in Marseilles is so French it's impossible to get anything done, especially in English. The operator would always say, "Ah oui, ah call you back een one hour."

Four hours later we'd call her back and she'd say, "Ah oui, oui, ah call you back een one hour." Meanwhile everybody is screaming at each other in French and throwing wine bottles in the background. Then one night when Chris and I were sleeping two guys casually walked into the room, and turned on the light. We jumped up yelling, "YAHHHHHH!" They took off and we screamed over the telephone at the desk clerk to stop them, but they were just acting casual. They probably didn't know we were in the room.

There was a whole bunch of bratty belligerent boys standing in front of the stage at the Marseilles gig. They were going, "Nyuuh, nyuuh," making faces through the whole thing, so during the encore Chris and Jimmy dumped cups of honey all over them. Then we attacked, throwing microphone stands at them, but then this gorgeous little thirteen-year-old French girl, who was standing right next to them, screamed out and started to cry. After the gig she was

crying so hysterically the guards brought her back-stage, and the boys gave her their ties, or something like that. But the thing in Marseilles was that the electricity, like Bangkok's, had no ground. All the electricity in the hall came from two bare copper terminals that were jammed into the wall, and anyone who went near them could have died.

From Marseilles we went to Vienna where I finally got a flu shot. I know that people think being a rock star and playing to hysterical fans in theaters around the world is great, and it *is* a lot of fun being wined and dined around the world, but by then every time we'd go out to some fabulous dinner we'd be dying of battle fatigue.

From Vienna we dragged on into Germany. Every time we went through German customs there was the same tall bald Prussian customs official with a mono-cle who would go through our stuff. We did a lot of TV shows during this tour. We played Munich, Hamburg, and Berlin, went on to Sweden and finally went back to England, where we did some more promo work, made some videotapes, and played a few more gigs. When we first went to England we were no-bodies. We could check it out and see what was happening, but it got harder as we became better known. "Denis" was a No. 1 hit single. Also the pop fans in England are attracted to pop stars and if one is going to be available for an autograph session they'll hear

Debbie and Julietta Messina.

Paris.

Frankie and Debbie, after hearing news of the cancelled gig, Bordeaux.

Marseilles.

At Checkpoint Charlie. Roadie Michael Sticca is at far right.

Hotel Berlin.

124

about it on the radio and show up in droves. We had over 500 people at a record store no bigger than my living room, and it's small. We were downright popular in England. Apart from the singles, the record company had built up our image with a lot of photographs and press that preceded our return. The photographs are very important. They made my face into an archetype, and identified each member of the band. That hadn't existed before we arrived back from the world tour, and certainly hadn't been happening in Japan where we still had to grovel to get on the cover of a magazine. This was when the first article about Blondiemania appeared in *Sounds*. We were played on the radio constantly and glossy pictures of me flooded the marketplace. It was all starting to peak. However, some of the press had built us up from the first album, so now they were ready to cut us back down for the second one. We did a number of what seemed to us pleasant interviews, which would then in print say what fucked-up monkeys we were in five-page putdowns saying we sucked. This resulted in our refusing interviews for various publications. We thought people were being friendly when they were looking for a chance to be rotten.

Before returning to the States we went to the famous Sid Vicious gig at the Electric Ballroom in London. It was a do-or-die show, saved from the depths of depravity by an excellent sound system and Rat Scabies' magnificent playing. We finally left with Joan Jett, Sandy West, Eddie the Ant, and various others. Drunk to the point of insensibility we all accepted a free ride in the back of a moving van. The door slid closed, and the thing hurtled through the dark streets like a gigantic tin can. Inside everyone went loco, screaming and kicking the walls, bouncing off the floor and rolling around like a bunch of freaks. The roar of metal walls being beaten was deafening. Joan and Eddie (who did most of the beating) collapsed exhausted as the truck screeched to a halt outside our flat in the Kings Road. A week later Clem pointed out a small item in the press about Blondie in all their capitalist glory leaving the Sid Vicious gig in a limousine.

Everybody in America should get a free world tour. It would be reasonable to send everybody around the world once. They're only going to waste their money in other ways if they don't go. Nobody gets any sense of anything until they see the Third World and the communist countries in person. It's certainly disillusioning as far as any ideals you might have about communism and leftwing semantics are concerned. That's finished when you get into any communist countries; it's all bullshit. There's no political camaraderie except to survive. Everybody's totally paranoid. It's just like the movies. And the Third World countries are wrecked. We weren't in Africa so I don't know about that, but this trip around the world did just confirm the evil I think is out there. The good aspects are few and far between. If America's the best place in the world, then we're all in bad shape.

We flew to Germany to do a TV show and then took a very long disjointed plane ride back to the States, during which we had to spend ten hours waiting in a German airport. After this six-and-a-half-month world tour we were surreal. We taped the ten hour airport background noises. No one said anything because we were all too burned out to notice.

Packing.

Fans waiting in sun.

Fans waiting in rain.

PARALLEL LINES

PARALLEL LINES

Back in New York we checked into the Gramercy Park Hotel completely exhausted and disoriented. It was the end of February, 1978. Everybody had been promised a month off after the world tour and we gratefully fell into bed looking forward to thirty days and nights of sleep, but before I could unpack, my sister called to say Sunday Man had run away while I'd been gone. I cried for hours. Later, Terry Ellis called and said nobody in America was playing our records because the DJs and programmers who control what the kids hear thought we were punks, which was a no-no. Furthermore, although we had two albums and singles that had been hits in Europe and Asia, and had just toured the world for over six months, we hadn't made any money at all. They explained to us that if we didn't break in America we wouldn't make enough money to buy shoes let alone cover our expenses. This sounded completely ridiculous, but we had no idea whether it was true or not, and no way of finding out.

Terry Ellis wanted me to go on a U.S. promo tour with Peter Leeds so all the DJs and press could meet me, at which point, he theorized, they would immediately play our records. We thought MacDonalds should manage us and sell a record with every burger. It seemed obvious to us that the radio would play all our hit singles like "Denis Denis," "Presence Dear," and "In The Flesh," but they still weren't and I was told if I didn't do this promo tour Blondie would be dead. After working so hard this news seemed impossible to bear, but it was explained to us in detail that it was true. You cannot imagine how confused and tired we were. Finally I agreed to leave almost immediately on yet another series of disorienting plane rides on the condition that Chris accompany me instead of Leeds, because relations between Leeds and us were already strained to the breaking point. It was only a matter of time before we would separate irrevocably. My assignment was to talk to a bunch of people who didn't want to play our records about why they should. I had to explain punk, a vague media image they had helped create but were not able to define. After this they would supposedly see I/we weren't what they thought.

Before we left New York I saw a very deep and meaningful picture called *House of Horrors*. This 1946 "B" epic features not only a great story line but one of the most unusual film stars of all time: Rondo Hatton.

Hatton made famous the role of "the creeper" for Universal studios. The creeper is a giant, ugly, man-like monster. Interestingly enough Rondo never had to put on any make-up for his role. Poor Hatton was afflicted with a rare glandular disease called acromegaly, which made him look like "the creeper." He made several films for Universal, generally portraying homicidal maniacs, but he died shortly after completing *The Brute Man* (the third creeper film) in 1946.

House of Horrors may be Hatton's greatest role. Not only does Rondo spend more time on screen, and speak more lines, but the film has an important message. Read on:

Actor Martin Kosleck plays a mad sculptor. Martin is about to make a sale to an important buyer, but wait, the buyer is accompanied to the sculptor's studio by (you guessed it) the evil, malicious, arrogant, powerful critic! The critic hates modern art and in no uncertain terms tells the buyer not to waste his money or time on such crap. Martin goes wild and chases them both out with a kitchen knife. The next day the critic writes a twenty-page piece on Martin's lack of talent, why bother, etc., etc., in a biting and vicious attack. That evening as Martin goes to the river to drown himself he notices a figure unconscious on the shore. He rescues Rondo and needless to say they become fast friends.

Martin forgets about doing himself in and is soon absorbed in sculpting Rondo's head, but he can't forget the miserable critic who persists in tearing him apart in print on a regular basis. As Martin reads yet another horrendous review he rants and raves in endless semi-poetic jargon about the injustices of life and the futility of it all. Rondo absorbs all this and then delivers his best line: "You don't like the guy, do you?" Martin then does twenty minutes of poetic analysis on Hatton's understatement and is too busy talking to notice his departure. Guess where Rondo goes? He goes to the critic's house and pounds him to a pulp as he sits at his typewriter.

And therein lies the message for us all! Woe be it that all artists have their own pet Rondo, a sort of opposite muse, the ugly god of the id—for every time Martin got a bum review, out would trot old Rondo to rend and shred the reviewer. But where did it get him? Better yet where did it get the critics? And finally, would Rondo Hatton have noticed if he got a bad review?

In each city a Chrysalis sales rep would convey me through a series of meetings with DJs at radio stations, press interviews, and visits to distributors and stores. Billy Bass was their midwestern rep. We started hanging out with him in Detroit. He knew and was known by a lot of these people and he told us some of the rules of the game, so he got us operating on a more instinctual level and made everything

American Airport.

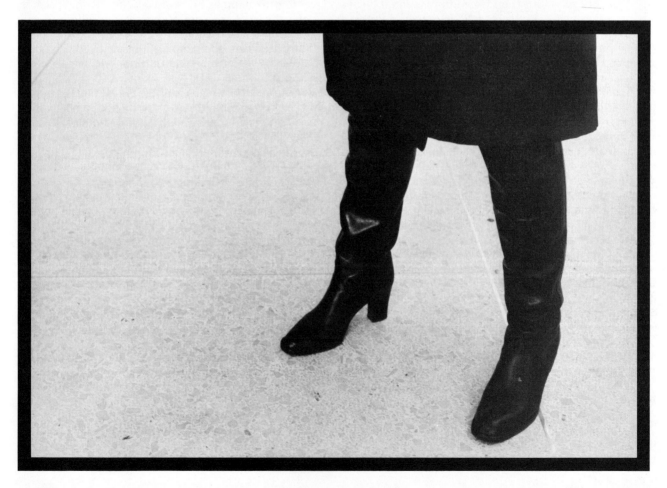

Debbie and Ray Davies.

very pleasant. He had been one of the main forces in breaking David Bowie in America; now he was playing a starring role in helping break Blondie across the country.

Chrysalis wanted me to front the group alone so all the press attention would be focused on me, because they still thought that I was our strongest asset and attention drawer, so I found myself talking to people—some of whom turned out to be truly great fans from the start, but some who didn't know anything about me—coast to coast. Knowing very well that none of these people had any reasons to be afraid of me, and noticing that some of them were, I realized they were afraid of themselves and using their illusions of me to blame their fear on an outside force, so they wouldn't have to contend with it. In the same way people "blame" blacks, Puerto Ricans or Cubans, they were "blaming" punks for causing social unrest with diseased attitudes.

I have a certain amount of fear inside me, and I always try to find out what causes it so I'm not confused. People should make a conscious effort to deal with their own fears and stop blaming them on other people. However, I think one of the main reasons I did finally break through to the audience in the States, that we knew would like us if we could get to them, was specifically because I'm not the wild violent girl of the Australian press's dreams. The con-

nection I make with the audience calms people down, which is good.

By the end of the promotion tour I began to see that programmers and DJs were opening up to us, they just didn't know what to play. They kept saying, "We like you. Give us something to play." I didn't understand why they couldn't play "Denis Denis," or "Presence Dear," or "In The Flesh."

Back at the Gramercy Park we were getting ready to make *Parallel Lines.* Chris wrote "Sunday Girl" one afternoon when he missed me and Sunday Man. I was away doing more promo and the cat had never returned. In May the Gramercy Park wouldn't give us the same low monthly rate any more so we moved to the Southgate Towers opposite Madison Square Garden. At this point Chrysalis and Leeds started paying us salaries of $125 a week each from the advance on our next record. A fortune. At last we thought we were beginning to make it, although we still hadn't seen a penny from *Blondie, Plastic Letters,* or any of the tours.

In May we played the Starwood in L.A., Mabuhay Gardens in San Francisco, and the Palladium in New York. The Palladium shows were great. Everyone would get stoned and crazy. We first met Robert Fripp when he came backstage at the Palladium. We did the Johnny Blitz benefit with him at CBGB's. Blitz was a member of the Dead Boys who almost got

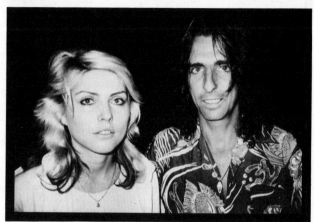

Debbie and Alice Cooper.

killed in a knife fight. Among many other acts, one that stands out in memory is Anya Phillips's strip-tease number. She was supposed to have a blackout and disappear when she was finished, but the lighting man was so entranced he forgot to turn the lights out. Everybody was staring at her, so she just ran off and got dressed in the kitchen. Fripp was making his first public appearance in some time, and he was also spectacular. In addition to our regular material we did Iggy's "Sister Midnight" and Donna Summer's "I Feel Love." It was a super gig and someone said afterwards that our sound put them in a trance. What could be better? I always wanted to play trance rock. Around this time Chris met Walter Stedding, another trance rocker, and invited him to open for us at CBGB's. Walter played violin along with his biofeedback machine, which he plugged into his brain. Chris and he soon started making tapes together.

In June we went into the studio to make *Parallel Lines* with Mike Chapman producing. The first things he said to us were, making an album is a nine to five job, and you don't want to record anything you're going to be embarrassed about ten years from now. He's a perfectionist. We weren't prepared for his level of expertise so we learned an enormous amount about how to record from him. His approach was very different from Gottehrer's. Chapman helped us

become more commercial, with tighter arrangements and perfect basic tracks. He worked with his engineer, Pete Coleman, whom he's trained from birth. We were very pleased with the arrangement because we wanted a No. 1 record in America and that's also what Chapman wanted. We knew he was as happy about working with us as we were with him, so this new collaboration was exciting from the beginning.

Chris had written "Fade Away and Radiate" in 1974. Robert Fripp contributed a lot to the psychedelic sound on the track, recorded in 1978. He plays really quietly and it completely changes the atmosphere. "Heart of Glass" was a funky James Brown type song we wrote on Thompson Street in 1975. I remember Chris lying on the bed strumming those chords endlessly. Sometimes I had to fight for space on the bed—it was me or the guitar—but after a while I got my own bed and made up the lyrics. That's how we wrote the song.

When we did "Heart of Glass" it wasn't too cool in our social set to play disco, but we did it because we wanted to be uncool. Mike was conducting us as we played; there was a lot of eye contact. The emotions were more intense on that album. "Heart of Glass" was based around a Roland Rhythm Machine and the backing took over ten hours to get down. We spent three hours just getting the bass drum. It was the hardest song to do on the album and took us the

Hotel life.

longest in studio hours. Chapman was concentrating on getting it mechanical.

On the first album we didn't know what we were doing. We just went into the studio and did it. Gottehrer had his hands full. On the second album we didn't have a regular bass player. On *Parallel Lines* the quality of musicianship had definitely gone up. Blondie was now six people who had been playing live together continuously for a year, which makes a big difference in itself. Early one July morning, after an all-night session, Pete Coleman and Mike Chapman carried seven reels of tape out of the studio, got a taxi to the airport, and flew to California to mix.

The title is especially significant. It comes from a song we didn't have time to finish, but we used the name about communications, characterization, and the eventual meeting of different influences, and it was the same initials as the second album *Plastic Letters*. My only reservation is that the cover stinks. The stripes design was Leeds's idea and he gave us the impression that we were going to be fading in and out of the stripes, which we liked. We had no idea we were going to be standing in front of them, and we didn't know the logo was going to be ripped off from a Blimpie's logo. Leeds wanted the boys to smile and me to frown on the cover. None of us wanted to be smiling, but he managed to get everyone to take one picture smiling. He said, "Oh, let's just take one any-

way." One day we went to his office and there was a polaroid of the cover nonchalantly lying on his desk. We said, "What the fuck is this?" And Leeds said, "It's the cover." Everybody flipped out and yelled, "These are the wrong pictures," because we'd carefully picked out the pictures of ourselves we wanted and these were different. That was pretty much the last straw for everybody with him.

After the album we warmed up for our July–August tour with The Kinks. We played Santa Cruz, San Diego, Phoenix, Kansas City, Minneapolis, St. Louis, Austin, Dallas, Houston, Detroit, Toronto, Atlanta, and Miami. The press were still asking if we were punks or not and I was getting too tired of it. Blondie is a pop band and we told that to everyone who would listen. This punk label, which was a media creation, was doing a lot of bands harm by distracting from their exhilarating music. We'd achieved success and acceptance in almost every record market in the world; *Plastic Letters* was a hit in Europe, "Denis" was No. 1, but we still weren't getting anything like that kind of acceptance in the States, although we could see it coming gradually.

With *Parallel Lines* under our belts but not in the stores yet we were trying to reach a broader audience and it began working on this tour, because as more and more people saw us, DJs started playing some of our stuff, and we got more support from the press.

131

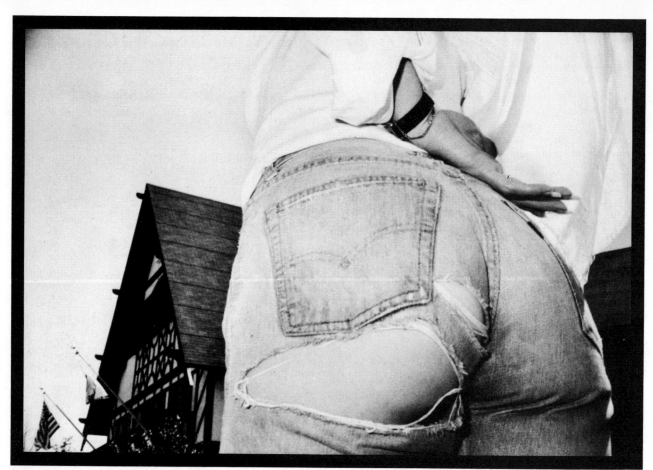

Early jeans ad.

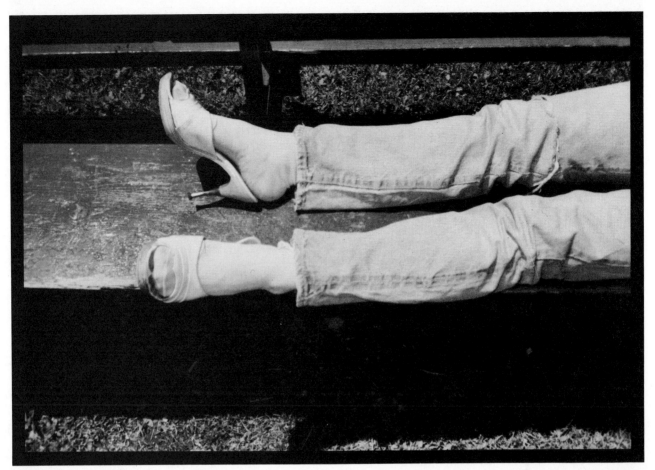

Debbie's feet.

Rare indoor UFO shot, Pennsylvania.

133

Debbie and The Buzzcocks.

Everyone realized we were there to entertain them, not attack them, and the country gradually began opening up. We got a lot of good press in the South and West and began to see that we could break America if we kept at it.

The Kinks were fun to work with, helpful and friendly rather than competitive, so we appreciated that. There was more of a split in the music than we'd experienced with Iggy or Television, but the audience accepted us.

HEART OF GLASS EUROPEAN TOUR

By the end of the tour *Parallel Lines* was being released worldwide and we went straight on to Europe. "I'm Gonna Love You Too" was the first single released in the U.S. and it hadn't done anything. Then they released "Hanging On The Telephone" and it was a No. 1 hit when we went to the U.K. This chaotic tour began at Bilzen where we played a festival in front of ten thousand people for $20,000. It was the biggest audience, the most amount of money we'd earned to date, and one of the worst gigs we ever did. Since we'd gone directly from The Kinks tour to Europe the equipment had been shipped from a concert

in the U.S. to this concert in Europe, and much of it had gotten broken in the process. Consequently, during the concert our instruments constantly malfunctioned. Keith Crabtree, The Flying Roadie, helped save the day by running around patching things up, but everyone was uncomfortable and afterwards a riot broke out backstage.

We went to London and stayed in some rent-a-flats on the Kings Road at World's End for a week. The Miranda Gallery did a photo show called Blondie in Camera. The British press were at the height of their frenzied political interpretation of rock music. We told them in the interviews we did at the time that you cannot create social change with political music in America now. Everybody in England was talking about the political stands of The Sex Pistols and The Clash.

Politics is business—getting enough money to win, keeping enough to stay in power and make more as a politician. The politicization of art in the sixties was very hypocritical. It existed in the minds of the people who wanted it to exist, but the people who were in power were definitely not having anything to do with it.

I don't think there's too much difference between the American and British scenes. Everybody wants the same things for themselves and their culture, but the methods have to be different because of the

Dutch T.V. show.

differences in the way the cultures operate. In America Iggy was a radical force without saying anything political. His presence and what he did was a radical phenomenon. If somebody can get on a subway and wipe out the minds of the people who see him, he's having an effect on them and doesn't need to say anything. I hope the kids in England realize that we all want the same things, we're just going about it in different ways.

By the time we went back to Europe to tour with *Parallel Lines* our experiences had given us a different outlook on touring. The combination of our explosive relations with Leeds and our still being completely broke while being famous and successful, was making living and working very difficult. This was the most abrupt and disruptive transitional period for us. Our problems with Leeds greatly dampened the excitement of touring.

Our values went through a terrible shake-up and we often wondered, Is all this really worth it? because I could be just as happy having a little band and running around doing club dates, making enough money to pay the rent and buy pizza every now and then. However, one positive thing about being in rock'nroll and being forced into ugly business situations is that through all this, if you can survive and continue, when you do have a chance to play your music it becomes so important to you because it pro-

vides a wonderful relief in a private world. The funniest thing is, the music is the reason all the other bullshit exists.

Things with Leeds got worse and worse. We discovered he had changed the schedule of the tour from what we had agreed upon in New York. Chris finally confronted him about this and everything else during a long fight over the phone in London. First he told Chris that he was too busy to tell us about the changes in our schedule and simply couldn't be bothered. Later in the same conversation he said Chris was stupid because he had told him the changes had been made and Chris had forgotten. He was still treating us like kids. He knew we weren't that dumb but he couldn't bring himself to treat us as equals. The old saying barefoot and pregnant paralleled our situation of on the road and ignorant. Plus he had us pretty neatly tied up contractually so he didn't really care anyway. We finally flipped out completely after another couple of fights about how he wasn't keeping us informed before locking us into obligations. Chris called our lawyer in New York, to whom we'd already given copies of all our contracts, and he told us it was written in the contract that we didn't have to pay Leeds's traveling expenses on tour. We told him that we weren't obliged to do so and, since we didn't want him around, weren't going to.

So there we were, stuck on this tour with no man-

Dutch T.V. show.

Hippie concentration camp, Belgium.

136

Debbie and Frankie, Dutch T.V. show.

Debbie and Fripp.

ager or tour manager from August 26–September 24. The Buzzcocks opened for us. We played Sweden, Germany, Holland, Belgium, Holland, and England. The Boyfriends opened for us on the English gigs. We brought Eddie "The Ant" Dugan along with us. He came out at the end of "Attack of The Giant Ants" in an ant costume made of a football helmet with antennae, and attacked me on stage. It worked out well, except sometimes the roadies would rush out, strip him and throw him naked into the audience, or tape him to the microphone with gaffer tape and just leave him out there at the end of the show. The days of just hanging out on Kings Road in London with punk kids were over. In between shows I was always working doing photo sessions or press. I did get to see some bands. After England we went to Germany and Switzerland. That tour was pretty sleazy. Our backdrops and rugs were stolen. Again, we never saw a cent.

BACK IN THE U.S.A.

We came back to the States at the end of September, 1978. The flight was pretty lousy, the plane was small, it took eight hours, and there was no movie,

but coming back to New York is always stimulating. The cars suddenly get longer and you notice teenagers don't ride motorcycles. We had a month before touring the States. We moved into our current apartment where we are making this book. That was a big help after living in hotels since 1977. During this period we hardly had time to unpack our suitcases let alone take anything out of storage. Chris couldn't lay his hands on his photography for over a year. It was frustrating.

When we came back to the States at the end of the *Parallel Lines* tour we felt opinions beginning to change because now "Heart of Glass" (the third single off *Parallel Lines)* was climbing the American charts. A lot of people we'd hung out and been close friends with on the scene for years said we'd sold out by doing a disco song. This is a blatantly ridiculous statement. It always pissed me off that people could have the nerve to pretend to be so stupid. We'd been consciously looking for a sound to break into American radio, and "Heart of Glass" was one of the most innovative songs Blondie recorded. If it hadn't been a hit nobody would have said anything about it, except maybe, "Oh, Blondie did a disco song, isn't that cute." The reason it's a hit is because it's a good song. We used to do it in 1975 as a funk song; we simply changed the arrangement and feel. Its Euro-disco sound—a cross between Kraftwerk and Giorgio Mo-

Back in New York.

rodor—was novel then. Marty Thau told us he was at a disco convention when he first heard it and thought, This is really hip, it's punk-disco, not having realized that it was us. It has a syncopated sound. We like Donna Summer and The Bee Gees' disco songs. That stuff is good if you're open-minded and don't make a big political deal out of it. With me it's a psychic thing that has to do with the beat. The 4/4 heartbeat rhythm has a calming effect on the listener. It's popular because it's biological.

The first thing we did to set matters right with Leeds was try in good faith to renegotiate our contract, but that was fruitless as he stood firm. We knew we had to get divorced. There was no reason to renegotiate since he had us all neatly tied up legally to his advantage. By this time we had Bert Padell, our business manager, and Marty Silfen, our lawyer, giving us rational legal advice.

From October 29–November 16 we did a three-week tour of the States, doing two shows a night with different groups opening for us in different parts of the country. We kicked it off with David Johansen opening for us at Glassboro State College. Elvis Costello joined him for an encore.

I'm always nervous before I go on and I hope I always will be. It rushes me right out onto the stage. Scared shit is not just a joke. At this time we were getting fees in the range of $2,000 per show. We played Long Island, Boston, Philadelphia, Buffalo, Cleveland.

Notes taken driving into Cleveland from the airport November 11, 1978: The heartland, the home of de-evolution, the psychic center of American Desperation—Cleveland is gray and brown. Warm gray in the summer and frozen solid for what seems like endless winter. The grass and trees are gray. The roads are broken from severe temperature changes. Dante's Inferno of steel mills stretches for miles like glowing hell. Belching flames and sulphurous smoke are beautiful in a macabre way. The steel mills employ the people, and in return destroy the environment.

We enter the city. It's flat, brown and gray, the streets seem empty. No neon blaze lights the eye, a plain city, clean lines ravaged by fifty years of hard mid-American winters. Lake Erie is a frozen mirror for a giant.

Stiv Bators, Dead Boy, lives in Cleveland sometimes. He grew up there. "You shouldn't walk around the streets," he told us. At night? "Never. Everyone goes out in cars. If you walk you're a victim. Someone drives by and throws a beer can at you, or gets out of their car and jumps on your head. When we drive around we throw beer cans at victims, it's part of the culture; you have to mess with pedestrians."

Parks, hills, and bridged waterways separate huge masses of rich and poor whites and blacks. Racial

139

Legs and his parents.

tensions run high and the white power store on Clark Avenue is something of a tourist attraction. Lurid Nazi regalia, American flags, and religious icons are absurdly combined in anti-black hysteria. Across the street F.B.I. agents with big binoculars make their presence known on a regular basis. In the middle of this devastation is downtown Cleveland which contains the Cleveland rock scene and Swingos Hotel. Swingos is famous. It may be the most music oriented hotel in North America. Perhaps every soul band and half the rock bands in the world have stayed here. Here Cheetah Chrome pushed a soda machine through a wall onto a screwing couple. Iggy and Bowie have held court here for Blondie and The Runaways, Alice's snakes got lost in the lobby. Swingos has seen them all. The rooms are decorated in a tacky bachelor-pad chrome, with black and red rugs, subdued lights, and peeling paint. We heard screams in the night, howls in the halls, and saw festivity, coke dealers in Cadillacs, life in the middle of decay: Swingos in Ohio in the great blue American night is the heart of rock'nroll in Cleveland.

Sunday we flew back to New York and played the Palladium that night. Mitch Ryder and The Detroit Wheels opened for us. Tuesday we went up to Shelton, Connecticut, to play the Pine Crest Country Club and Wednesday, November 15, we were in Hartford at Toad Hall. When you're a rock singer on tour, you're expected to behave in a clichéd way. This is how the world is going to know who you are. That's bullshit. I'm against the idea that rock stars have to live a life that's completely understandable or predictable. Maybe I'll just be the mysterious figure that'll never be able to be truly defined. We played New Haven, and then went out to the West Coast and played San Francisco, Santa Cruz, and Santa Monica.

Fripp told us he had been informed that President Carter actually said, "Boys, we really don't want New Wave," to a group of leading record executives. We believe this. It seemed obvious to us as we toured the States in November that somebody in control was stopping New Wave music from being played on the radio. The Ramones "Rockaway Beach" had just come out and wasn't getting anything like the airplay it deserved. Our audiences were responding extraordinarily well at our concerts, but we still weren't getting played on the radio in a big way.

The kids are always aware of what's new and they love it, but the machine still wasn't behind us even though *Parallel Lines* had been out for four months. We did get a lot of reviews and by the end of that tour the radio was beginning to play us, but "Heart

Amos Poe films the Invisible Man.

Joey Ramone outdrinks John Cale.

of Glass" wasn't No. 1 until six months after the album's release. The truth is that by the end of this tour in November, 1978, despite our widely based international success, and three albums, we were still having quite a bit of trouble getting airplay in the States.

We continued business negotiations and this was when we interviewed the forty managers. Bert Padell insisted we talk to a lot of different prospective managers, which turned out to be quite a revelation to us. We noticed how many of these guys were seeing us with a subjective understanding, which was Bert's point in making us talk to as many types of businessmen as possible.

We didn't know exactly what we wanted in a manager because we'd never really had one. Being a manager is a strange job because it's such an intangible thing. There's a different function to perform in every case. Any manager that comes up and says, "I am the best manager for you," is full of shit. It's like saying, "I am the best scientist." We knew that we needed someone who was not just a mercenary opportunist who wanted to work a rock band to the ground in order to make a few million dollars, or whatever it was that could be made out of Blondie as a touring/recording band.

When we met Shep Gordon we picked up on him

right away. We'd done a couple of gigs with Alice Cooper, which had been fabulous as we naturally were Alice fans, and we knew what Shep had done for Alice. They came up together. Shep is an honest person and he likes to hear ideas from his acts instead of being mega-manager. The main thing is, he's very tasteful, and he only does things he's interested in. We picked him over the other forty managers because he didn't say, "I am going to make you five million dollars in the first two weeks. I'm terrific and I am going to do the best job."

Shep said, "I'm interested and if you want me to do it, I will." And he didn't want a contract, whereas practically all the others wanted big solid binding five-year contracts with options. That was another major incentive to go with him because here was a man who was genuinely going on a trust relationship. Everything Shep has worked with has been successful. When Chris and I initially talked to him we said we felt Blondie had a certain limit to making money because touring was always such a problem for us.

New Year's Eve 1978-1979 we played Winterland in San Francisco with REO Speedwagon. Winterland was closing that month. Only a few more shows and it was going to be torn down. Bill Graham opened Winterland with the Jefferson Airplane in the flower days and long after the demise of the Filmore East

Arturo Vega.

and West, Winterland thrived. Inside, it was an old echoey theater with a similar vibe to the Roundhouse in London, but about 2,500 seats bigger.

The day of the show Blondie went on KSAN radio and Clem told the audience they should leave after we played (before REO came on). Oh oh . . . Word drifted back to the Blondie camp that REO's lead singer had heard the broadcast from the confines of his limo and was ready to kill. Tension mounted.

Would they turn off the sound and lights during the first song? Would Clem be shot during the second song? Fears turned out to be unfounded, however, and the only hint of revenge was Blondie being hustled off with only a bow, leaving the crowd howling for an encore. It was one of our greatest American gigs. The crowd went wild. Afterwards we got the royal San Francisco treatment: we were invited to the Jefferson Airplane's black mansion where we met John Belushi and a vast assortment of music and TV personalities. Later that night at an Avengers gig at the Mabuhay Gardens a fight involving 200 people broke out, tables and bodies went flying and blood flowed, but no one was seriously damaged and the Avengers finished their set in relative peace. It was the night of the full moon.

When we got home to New York Chris went to one of the meetings between Leeds and Marty Silfen as these business changes were being made, but then we

decided to let the lawyers sling the shit back and forth until the mess was cleaned up. Because rock'n roll artists are young they're taken for a terrific ride. They're the most used people in any art form in the world because they work very hard physically for long hours and nine times out of ten by the time they get to the point where they should have made something, they discover they've been ripped off.

Finally, "Heart of Glass" looked as if it was actually going to become a big hit in the States. Everybody said, "Oh, you're so lucky," but every week it was going up the charts Peter Leeds and his lawyers were saying, "Look, it's up to No. 17, they're getting more famous, so the divorce settlement is going to cost *more* money." Consequently we couldn't enjoy our success very much at that point. In fact it was a heartache. We were going "Ohh ohh, too bad it's a hit now, if we'd only waited, if only it wasn't a hit." It was a drag. Finally, after all the smoke had cleared, we agreed to buy Leeds out of the contract. Once again we paid our way out. The experience was gross and disillusioning. Leeds made more money out of Blondie than any other single person. It affected our attitudes about whether anything was very fair or not, and took a long time to get over.

Whatever, at least Blondie was on its own two feet so to speak and finally considered legitimate airplay music. We were being invited to perform on Mike

Hotel life.

Douglas, Merv Griffin, Johnny Carson, Dick Clark, Midnight Special—all of them wanted us simultaneously. So now we were doing what we do for TV.

Blondie dresses like an urban band and has an urban beat, but I met a few cowboys that liked to listen to us. I love country music. The mass communications media have created codified structures, whereby everything is labeled concisely and within the dictates of fashion, which leaves audiences and performers alike holding the short end. Basically it blocks audiences from being able to hear what's being played. Programmers and DJs must sell ads so music is sent out in a limited format. Oftentimes the new sounds on radio have been played live in clubs for a year or more.

I started getting a few movie scripts. Needless to say I always wanted to be a "movie star." It's the good old American dream, but Chris always wanted to write movie music, too. I'd been in a few films by Amos Poe *(Black Generation, Unmade Beds,* and *The Foreigner),* plus we'd done hours of TV, but, as any actor/actress will tell you, it's very hard to get a good script. I got the scripts about nympho rock singers, whose managers have members of the audience killed for publicity, etc. After reading a number of these, I decided not to do a rock film. When we got the script for *Union City* we both liked it, and I was glad it was a low-budget independent project for me

to start with, so we talked to the director, Mark Reichert, and in February I made the movie.

The first day on the set I was so scared I was almost in tears. I thought, "I can't do it." I was shaking inside and out. Desperately trying to be rational, I said to myself, "You can't let this happen. You have to do it. What're you going to do? Quit?" I coaxed myself back into controlled panic with minor inner shakes. Then in the afternoon I studied the script and beat the words into my head, but I was having some trouble choreographing the words and movements to a camera rather than an audience.

Film has a different sense of timing and the pace is drier, intellectual and more personal. You don't have an audience response. You just do it. And if you do it well, you get turned on. There seems to be a very still, electrified atmosphere in film that can be equated to recording. When you're in front of the camera, and you're making this nonreality come alive on a piece of film, you can feel it. Something happens. We're all what we see ourselves as, and we're all what other people see us as, but a lot of times the thing we see ourselves as is much more complimentary than what reality is, or vice versa. Whatever that *is,* is what you have to produce on film.

The reason you have your picture taken in the first place is so other people can see it. When you're in front of a camera, there's the realization that you're

Iranian tour.

there because you want people to see you, and like you. It's also like being reassembled molecularly, because you are becoming whatever electricity and light are. Then when concentration is dead center there's a physical change, like when you're in the Concorde and you hit supersonic and the plane goes "huuuuh!"

If you're in front of a movie camera, one important thing to think about is the light. Are you using the light? Are you outside of your body and watching yourself? You become your own camera. I'm not an experienced actress yet, but I have a good sense of timing, and know how to use my light. It's almost an automatic instinct. I photograph well, and am able to project a certain personality, but at certain points I feel as if the scenes are happening to me, and it's a rush, like doing a show.

ZIPPING AROUND EUROPE AGAIN

After *Union City* we went on a two-week electronic promo tour of Europe because *Parallel Lines* was selling and more singles were coming off it. This was the most modern rock tour we ever did. We flew from country to country doing TV shows, which were broadcast to millions of people. We didn't play any live gigs. We did the hundredth performance of the top pop special in Germany and Holland with "Heart of Glass." It was economical, smart, efficient, and we thought it would be a breeze, but it was more work than regular touring. Our schedule moved us even faster from city to city. Sleep was down to five hours a night. "Get on the plane at nine A.M. The next morning! Yeah! We're off to Belgium, kids!" Every night we dined on great exotic European meals, so we ended up with low blood pressure, which makes it hard to wake up in the morning. We were now the biggest pop stars in Europe, zooming around in limousines to the best restaurants, but meanwhile we were totally zonked out and unable to eat, feeling like we were a hundred years old. Everything seems to balance out. You always pay for what you get. And as you get to know what the price is, you get a better idea of how far you want to go, and how much you want to pay.

When "Heart of Glass" hit No. 1 in the States, we were in Milan sitting in the bar of a beautiful hotel full of great Fellini hookers in black ostrich feather outfits waiting in the lobby for the Arabs. Somebody came down from upstairs where he had gotten a call from America saying it had actually reached No. 1. Everybody started toasting, laughing, jumping on the tables and screaming, but the Italians were nonplused at how happy we were acting.

144

Hotel still life.

FROM EAT TO THE BEAT
TO AUTOAMERICAN

Back in New York we did more TV appearances and made the videotape for "Heart of Glass" at New York, New York. In May we began recording *Eat To The Beat* at the Power Station, Commander Chapman at the controls for the second time. The Kinks were recording their new album in the studio next to ours, followed by Chic, so we met Nile Rodgers and Bernard Edwards. We didn't hang out together then due to our concentrated schedules. Bruce Springsteen was also there making *The River.*

We were becoming more adventurous about songwriting and playing, having had three years professional experience. We were looser in the studio now, tailoring the material for recording. We were also collaborating increasingly with Mike. He was suffering a lot during this album, on account of breaking up with his wife. Torturous phone calls from New York to Beverly Hills made the city harder than usual for him. Davie Tickle, his nineteen-year-old engineer, was, however, living it up nightly at Studio 54. He started going out with Cissy; then, in the middle of recording, switched to her identical sister, Missy. As

far as our participation in making *Eat To The Beat* is concerned, Chris wasn't there during the sessions except when absolutely necessary because he was moving back and forth between producing Casino Music, for ZE Records, and the Blondie record.

Everybody in the music industry gets jaded when listening to music every day on the job. This happens to fans, too. When you listen too much it becomes meaningless. Listening to music all day long is a different experience. I read a good book called *Through Music To The Self* in which the author said that if you were stuck on a desert island without hearing any music for a year, when you finally heard some, a dog food commercial would sound fantastic. Music is essentially important to people.

Even though most of American radio chose to ignore our first two albums, before picking up on *Parallel Lines* and the "Heart of Glass" single, we were already at a crossroads in our career. *Eat To The Beat* was our fourth album, though it was the first one that the American public had been waiting for. Billy Bass invented those little squares on the cover that were to be seen in every music ad for the next year.

By the time we finished it the band was organized and ready to spend July rehearsing for a short tour of the States with Rockpile, who seem to have long since broken up. Our business arrangements were still

145

Bert Padell.

in flux. Peter Leeds wasn't our manager any more but Shep Gordon hadn't completely taken over yet, so Bert Padell and Bruce Patron, our road manager, put our plans in action for the 1979 summer tour.

Bruce was one of the best road managers we'd had. Ironically he had applied to Leeds for the position earlier on, but Bruce was independent and headstrong, so Leeds didn't hire him. Bruce was efficient, but we harassed and tortured him from day one and he suffered a lot. However, the road manager's job is definitely to be tortured. Roadies are respected but a road manager has to suffer. He has to change flights five times a day, or change rental cars every day. It's a masochistic position, but Bruce enjoyed it.

Everything started out well with Rockpile. We took a balmy boatride with them in Tampa. Everyone from Rockpile was there with their girls and wives. Everybody from Blondie was there with their girls. We freed the boat from its moorings and set off on a midnight cruise. The cool southern guys were jumping in the water, but when Clem ripped all his clothes off and jumped in, he got attacked by so many jellyfish he jet-jumped out screaming, "Shit, shit," and stood around naked going, "Eeeuuggggh, shit."

We always got a great response. Sometimes it seemed ridiculously good. Yet my feelings were not as they had been during the world tour of '78. This was

probably because my energy was so well-directed and defined on stage that performing was surreally effortless, although I'd still be soaked with sweat by the end of each show. I went on feeling surreal. I would try to take the audience on the Blondie escapades and emotional voyages, and this worked very well for me. Nine times out of ten we would start with the older material working toward the end of the set to the newer material.

The group identity came out more, because, even though my position as vocalist on stage was more obvious, and the audience wanted more of me, I had to do less on stage. Blondie was a known group, with well-known material. My pre-show routine includes warming up, singing, and going over the set song by song, zeroing in and concentrating on a feeling for each one. Next thing you're on, pinpointing the songs directly at the audience. When you're an underdog you work harder, do more things to get an audience interested, since you don't know what's going to interest them, so you use more energy.

As far as the commercial American rock scene is concerned the music is mostly supposed to reflect affluence, good times, heartthrobs, Sex Gods and Goddesses, vicarious thrills, and being on the road. So I was still perplexed during this tour by journalists who said I was punk. A contradictory review said, "Well, Ms. Harry was not very aggressive and acted

146

Vincent Fremont, Vice President of Andy Warhol Enterprises, still on the job.

very timid and vulnerable and did not fulfill her tough punk image everyone expects at all." The stigma of the word punk could not be absorbed into American culture as representing anything positive. It held Blondie back for a long time. I never said I was tough. I always thought that people who categorized us nostalgia, "punk," or anything were out of their minds.

Images of Rondo filled our heads and sometimes we wished he was around to mash, shred, and pulp the thoughtless critic, but we restrained ourselves from summoning him up and pushed on. In place of Rondo, the even greater Tony Ingrassia, who'd moved to Berlin since working with us on "Vain Victory," came along as choreographer. We spent more time rehearsing with him, greatly improving our stage shows.

We stayed at some gargantuan ultra-modern hotels across the country on this tour. Remember the one where the balcony collapsed, killing seventy dancing couples? And in St. Louis there was the Alphaville Fantasy Hotel, jammed when we were there with the Young People's Christian Association Picnic, which was comprised of four thousand hysterically repressed Christian kids selling Christian T-shirts. It was like a beehive with a thousand identical rooms ranged around a vast circular corridor. When they finally pinned who we were, the kids

freaked out, went bananas, and ran around the star wars corridor past our rooms screaming and yelling. They had enough energy for twenty bands.

As the tour continued Rockpile started to become competitive, which is not a good way to operate when two bands are working on the road together. They should try to be homogeneous. I don't think they liked the idea of being an opening band, and particularly didn't like opening for me. Their manager, Jake Rivera, è uno macho, ha serrato nuestro organisatore de lo tour Bruce Patron que has estato fantastico poi ha provato a amasarlo davanti a tuto la trupe e ha veremente scoso Bruce.

At one gig we barred any photographers from coming backstage and Jake decided this was an insult to Rockpile. He rushed up and yelled in Chris's face, "YAAA you fucking guys, the photographers, bla bla." But by that time we were tour-zapped and didn't give a fuck what was going on. After the incident with the photographers things got progressively out of hand.

Rockpile did a hot show in San Francisco, but instead of turning on the lights after two encores, Bill Graham gave them four encores. On s'est alors vraiment fâchès apres lui mais à ce moment Bill Graham aussi essayé de tuer Bruce devant tous les roadies. By the last leg of the tour on the West Coast Shep Gordon's partner, Denny Vosburgh, who has a Wild Bill

In performance.

John Ferguson, our great English bodyguard.

Hickock mustache, very long hair, and is enormous, joined us and immediately cooled everyone out. We were beginning to benefit from Shep's management. A few gigs in California were played in outdoor arenas. By the time we got to L.A. we were enjoying ourselves—impossible but true. We discovered all the wacked-out hotels and Chris bought his first Jim Burns guitar in Indianapolis. This was also our western period when everybody got into cowboy clothes.

From the West Coast we went straight to Austin, Texas, to shoot our vignette in *Roadie,* a movie starring Meatloaf with guest appearances by us and Alice Cooper. Then we returned to New York to make the *Eat To The Beat* video disc.

The various scenes we've passed through have broken into millions of little splinter scenes. So the new scene we became involved in that was developing around Steve Mass's Mudd Club in Manhattan was a little piece of what happened before, but the people are more professional about their work than they were in the early glitter days, and it's a little more real because everybody has a chance to break through now. We continued seeing a lot of our friends and making new connections. Walter Steding, whom Chris was producing, was now being managed by Andy Warhol and playing with Lenny Ferrari. Glen O'Brien is a writer and TV talk show host who once had his own band called Konelrad. He started doing a

weekly cable TV show called Glen O'Brien's TV Party. Maripol, Edo, Amos Poe, Diego Cortez, James and Lisa Nares ran the cameras, and everyone in the scene went on that show. Chris was the co-host and Walter ('Doc') Steding's group was the band. Photographers on the scene like Willima Coupon, Bobby Grossman, Kate Simon, Marcia Resnick, Christopher Makos, Robert Mapplethorpe and the participants exhibited in Diego Cortez's fabulous PS 1 Art Show were among the guests on TV Party, too. By this time Anya Phillips had been managing a band for more than a year called the Contortions fronted by the fascinating and funky James White. We used to hang around and play with James sometimes. Chris was also working with Freddie Braithwaite, the graffiti artist who introduced us to rap music, and Snuky Taite. I could go on for pages. New York is full of people doing interesting things, and one of the major pleasures you can derive from the kind of celebrity success we'd attained is access to almost all of them.

Making the *Eat To The Beat* video disc was more fun than touring. Each day we were at a new location, working with the friends we were hanging out with. One day the whole gang came down to the Hoboken docks, we got dressed up like after-blast freaks and filmed "Atomic." "Dreaming" was released as a single in the middle of September and shortly thereafter *Eat To The Beat* came out. We had a bunch of No. 1 hits in

149

A rare photograph of Robert Fripp at home with Sister Fripp.

England and the rest of the world, but no No. 1's in the U.S. off that album.

In October the *Eat To The Beat* video disc, which was one of the very first rock album video discs, was released. David Mallet was the director and Chrysalis put it out in association with Alive Video, Inc. The Kinks had just come out with their video disc *One For The Road,* so after touring with them and recording next door to them, we were continuing to work in close parallels. During November and December Blondie rehearsed for their upcoming Christmas tour of England and Europe.

**EAT TO THE BEAT
EUROPEAN TOUR 1979–1980**

When we arrived in London mid-December, "Dreaming" was our fourth British No. 1 in two years. Three days later the Russians went into Afghanistan. That was creepy, now the tour was promising to be more bizarre than we'd anticipated. We rehearsed for a week in a cold drafty theater in an outlying London neighborhood. Joe Gannin directed the set-up of the show. We rehearsed with Eddie Gile, our lighting designer, incorporating Tony's ideas, too, and full sound. Before playing any concerts we did another in-store appearance in the same Our Price Records store on Kensington High St. that we'd done previously. This time three thousand fans came and the area was paralyzed. Traffic was backed up for blocks by crowds of zealots swarming into the street, while the police did their best to keep vehicles and pedestrians in order. I stuck my head out the upstairs window of the shop and the crowd cheered. Then Jimmy stuck his head out the window and yelled, "Do you wanna see her again?" Everybody went, "YEE-AAAHHHHH!" So I stuck my head out the window again and another cheer went up. I was plucked.

It's funny but I don't feel fragile in public situations. Arriving and leaving places we run across probably the worst crowd scenes. This is when bouncers and bodyguards come in handy. Sometimes it's the photographers, often adults, who start inching up to get a clear shot, who set off a chain reaction crush-in. I was in a situation where one bodyguard and I were surrounded by about fifty fans. John (bodyguard) is a mighty hunk of manpower but we were outnumbered. I said, "I'm gonna sign all the autographs, take your time, don't push." Those fans, excited as they were, didn't push, and I was impressed with how cool

Jim Burns in his shop.

they acted. For the most part people are pretty reasonable, because they don't want to get crushed anymore than you or I do.

We felt just like Beatlemania. In fact, we met Paul McCartney in front of our hotel as we were boarding our tour bus. He talked to Clem and asked Frankie if he was the drummer. We said, "Hello, nice to meet ya," to Paul and Linda, but Clem was ecstatic, shaking his head for twenty minutes afterwards. He couldn't speak. McCartney has always been his favorite pop star.

This last tour opened in Bournemouth (scene of our first British gig, Village Bowl, 1977) on December 26. We played the regular circuit of halls in Birmingham, Manchester, and Newcastle. There was a strong contrast between the short hot drives of America and the long cold drives of England, but this was a much hotter tour than the American one. It was wild the whole way. Everywhere we went there were mobs.

For New Year's Eve we returned to the Apollo in Glasgow, Scotland. That whole show was broadcast live by the BBC on TV and radio so everybody got to see or hear it. At midnight four members of the Strathclyde Pipers came out in full tartan regalia and played along on "Sunday Girl." In Scotland New Year's is called Hogmony. Everybody goes from house to house toasting the New Year, getting loaded, then sloshed and then knackered, etc., so the audience was in a celebrating mood, but the momentum of our Glasgow show, sacrificed in order to include all the songs the BBC wanted on the TV show, leveled the live show flat. No TNT finish.

That night after the gig one of our famous gigantic English roadies had a tremendous altercation with a famous gigantic Scottish guitar player and tried to kill him with a fire extinguisher. The celebrating roadie had gotten very drunk and the fight apparently involved the guitar player's girlfriend. They were rolling around in our quaint little hotel at three A.M. when the police arrived on the scene with the old Scottish detectives. We didn't have to talk to the police but we fed the huge English roadie Valiums so he would calm down. The next day Fat Frankie flew in from the States to replace him.

When we got to Edinburgh we were playing to a student audience in a lovely old hall. We were warmed up and groovy about to go on, when a piece of lighting equipment called a flashpot blew Eddie, our great lighting man, backwards across the stage in a blinding flash, leaving the audience so flabbergasted they sat stunned through the first half of our set. Eddie's was a hard act to follow. Luckily he was only scorched, not badly burned, although his burns did have to be wrapped in bandages. He had to be treated for shock and then returned home to the U.S. to recover. It was a miracle that his head was turned aside

151

An even rarer photograph of Pierre Salinger's nose, with Chris.

Fripp as Lemmy Caution, Debbie as Natasha Von Braun in the never made re-make of Jean Luc Goddard's Alphaville.
Hair by Mary Lou Green.

Debbie gets ready, Dallas, Texas.

Clem and Jimmy, London.

Steve Mass outside his Mudd Club, New York.

Debbie swims in the Pacific.

Debbie as King Tut. Make-up and art direction by Mary Lou Green.

as he bent over the flashpot, saving him from permanent blindness. Without Eddie's lights the show suffered immensely.

We also did two shows at a place called the Deeside Leisure Centre outside Liverpool, in a hockey-sized skating rink. It was packed with five thousand people, and the audience sang along on each song. Those two shows were the best gigs of the tour. By the time we got to London the tour tempo had pierced the ozone layer, but everything was so well-organized I could go onstage and deliver.

We continued to have enlightening experiences with the media. While we were in England and Paris, Barbara Lewis, a producer/director, got a free-lance commission from 20/20 to do a segment on the Blondie tour, shooting a total of twenty hours on the group. We did extensive interviews with Pierre Salinger in Paris, who at the time was also covering the Iranian hostage crisis. These twenty hours of footage were edited down to thirteen minutes. The questions they ended up using were safe pop questions that eliminated any possibility of helping anybody with similar experiences; i.e., all the serious things that were valuable to young kids were deleted. Of course, I don't mean to single out the 20/20 show. They did a fabulous piece on Blondie for the TV show, but the nature of TV doesn't leave room for taking risks.

The gig in Paris was funny because the schedule kept changing. First we were supposed to play a club and a theater. That fell through when the government closed the theater down. (The promoter hadn't paid his taxes.) We ended up playing in a circus tent in the freezing cold. No one got pneumonia but anybody who ate the seafood buffet backstage got violent food poisoning. We later heard another band got food poisoning from the same promoter, so we wondered whether he might be a mad poisoner of rock stars.

Denny Vosburgh came along with us on the entire U.K. tour. Shep also joined us briefly. By this time they knew from working with us how Blondie functioned as a touring band. Chris and I were talking to them about a number of outside projects we'd started to develop. Shep dug our ideas and respected our independence, as well as encouraging new adventurous moves.

The last shows of the tour were in London at the Hammersmith Odeon. These shows were also the last shows Blondie did to date. Our fans and friends in London and in all the U.K. made us a stellar response; in truth our British fans made us pop stars.

Since Blondie has stopped gigging for well over a year the many rumors of a split have arisen, subsided, come and gone. The question of the breakup of the group is always asked in interviews, and I have given the same answer whenever asked: No, we've not broken up.

I can only speak for Chris and me when I say this, but I felt we reached a plateau as a group. Touring limits opportunities like writing movie themes, producing other acts, making this book, etc. I didn't see my abilities leveling out, I see new challenges and I want to try them. So instead of blowing Blondie apart we've stretched out temporarily. I will admit to certain divisions within the band existing up to and through the last tour and I think cooling it is the answer. I love being Blondie, she's a part of me and I'm a part of it.

After the tour we spent a few days in London. Musical tastes and trends come and go very fast there. By then The Clash, Jam, and other groups we'd come up with were institutions and Blondie had become the most establishment type music. Underground in England the kids usually have terrific resentment toward established rock groups, but they still seemed to like us.

Before we left England Chris finally got a chance to meet Jim Burns, whose guitars he particularly favors. Burns has been making them since 1944. Chris was immediately attracted to a Burns-Scorpion he'd seen a photograph of in a magazine, because it reminded him of the Telecaster with two sets of horns he once carved up and painted black. Apparently Burns feels he's been fucked over by the system so much, having spent the bulk of his career designing guitars for other companies, that he told Chris his guitar is the Devil's guitar.

We flew back to New York on the Concorde. It's a thrill. Remember in those movies of the moon launch how the rockets jettison different parts? The plane feels like that when it shoots into a higher surge of power. The after burners go "thwoom," as it approaches space at the speed of sound, and everything is sort of nice. It made us want to be astronauts.

Fans saying goodbye.

Concorde pilots.

157

Debbie as honorary Frog Scout.

KOO KOO

When we got back to the States Giorgio Morodor got in touch with us about recording the theme song for *American Gigolo*. Paul Schraeder, who directed it, originally wanted us to do the theme song for the movie. We had gone to his hotel room and watched it on video cassette. A complex movie full of subtleties, it improves each time I see it. Schraeder linked us with Giorgio. The idea of our working together, unlikely in the first place because he was the king of disco and we were still the anti-establishment invaders from minimalist rock, proved to be excellent and controversial because Giorgio'd built up such a reputation and Blondie was the hot new thing on the scene at the time. He sent me a cassette tape of his music. His idea, direct and explicit, was to call it "Man Machine," the man being a professional gigolo, a sex machine. He had written some sample lyrics, but he wanted me to write something better.

American Gigolo has a fascinating high-tech visual including muted moody colors with subtle intensity, so the first verse, "color me your color baby," etc., came to mind at once as I listened to his music. It was teasing too, because in the movie he was always saying "Call me." "Call me if you want me to come to you." "Cover me." These little commands lent a demanding macho quality to being a male hooker. The first verse came fast and then the others followed easily.

We went back to the Power Station. Giorgio put down a synthesizer track in L.A. as a reference that was in perfect time, brought the tape to New York, and we all played along with that. Bruce Springsteen was still there making the same record eight months later. We thought that was pretty funny, but he's a nice guy and we saw a little of him. We cut the track in two days; first instruments, second vocals; it was like being a painter and working on commission.

Everybody knew and liked Giorgio's music so we weren't exactly surprised by how successful "Call Me" was. We thought it was a hit song when we first heard the demo. Getting Blondie together with Giorgio and having a hit song linked with the film was also very shrewd of Schraeder. And it was interesting for us to be involved with that sort of media event. This is a perfect example of a piece coming out of collaboration that is good for everyone. "Call Me" became our second No. 1 in America.

We had a certain sense of commitment to Blondie but after a while it was filled. We'd done everything we needed to get done—establishing the group, making sure everybody got paid, and making sure the records were out. Getting to do our own album covers and exactly what we wanted musically without hav-ing to make concessions had always been such a struggle for control. Control came with financial leverage and by *Eat To The Beat* we had complete control. We had also really got the concept of Blondie down to the extent that we didn't have to think about it or work on it that hard any more.

Since the Camaro was driven off a cliff we hadn't had a car. We didn't know whether to get a Japanese car to save on gas because of the oil shortage, or an American car to support American products and auto workers. We ended up choosing a Japanese car. This was fuel saving and since the corporation was owned more than likely by the C.I.A. we're backing American industry and saving on gas. To further support the cause we titled our next album *Autoamerican* and opened it with this statement:

> *Based on a desire for wasteful mobility and the serious physical pursuit of religious freedom, the auto drove mankind further than the wheel and in remote areas even today is forbidden as a device too suspect for human conveyance. This articulate conception has only brought us all more of the same. Thoughtlessly locked into phase two grid-lock, keyed up, on its rims and abandoned on the expressway.*

Around the time we bought a car we also started hanging out with Nile Rodgers and Bernard Edwards from Chic a bit more. They were in the Power Station almost constantly for years.

A lot of different things were keeping us happy in New York. We played with the Contortions at Hurrah's. Chris was in the studio with the Lounge Lizards and writing the score for *Union City*. We were working with Glen O'Brien. I did the Grammys with George Burns.

I was getting a number of offers to do commercials at the time. Since it was both lucrative and good exposure we decided to pursue one of these offers. Shortly thereafter Shep set up the deal with Murjani. We thought doing a jeans ad was funny, because in those days you couldn't turn on the TV without seeing a pair of designer jeans. Jeans seemed a natural, like rock'nroll, like apple pie. So we jumped on the bandwagon, with the understanding that we'd have full artistic control of the commercials.

When we got interested in the deal Warren Hirsch was the president of Murjani. Six months into the deal, after we had done our first commercial that was under our own creative control, Warren left the company. To me, the way you know if a commercial's successful is if you see a million other commercials that copy it. In England there were five different commercials with blondes walking down rainy streets

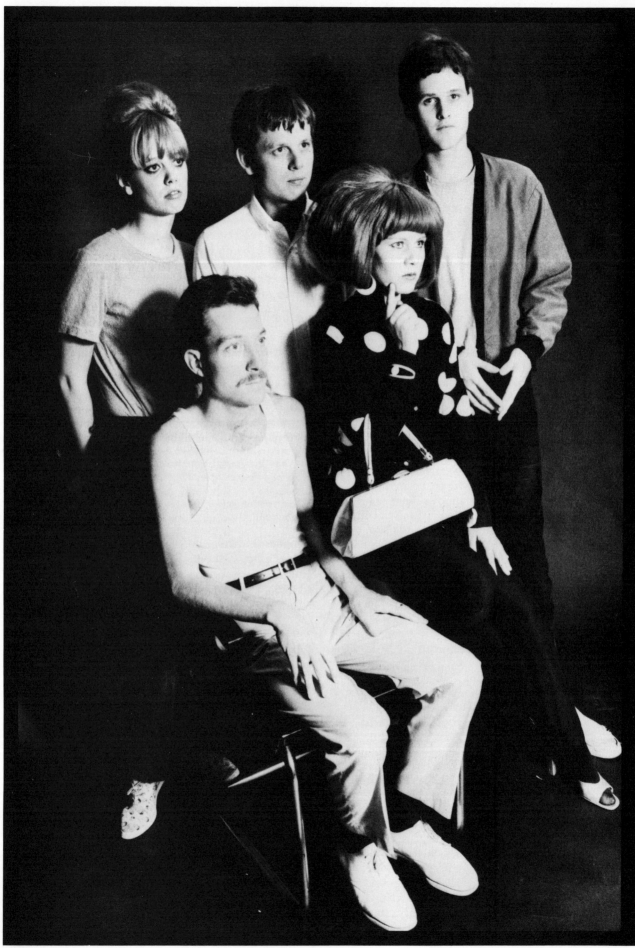

B-52s.

Chrissie Hynde, Pauline Black of Selector, Debbie, Poly Styrene, Viv from The Slits, and Siouxsie Banshee.

and there've been at least two copies in the States.

I think one of the major reasons we were successful in the first place was that everything we did was natural. We were never forced, like these groups that have one hit and the next thing they know they're playing in football stadiums to fifty thousand people. There was always a process of gradual build-up with us. The thing with the group just reached a certain level where everybody was definitely heading in different directions. Jimmy was producing a compilation album of new groups. Nigel was playing with Michael Des Barres's new band, Clem was producing the Colors, Chris was taking the Lizards' tapes to record companies, and producing Walter Steding's single "The Joke."

These different directions were exhibited on *Autoamerican*.

AUTOAMERICAN

In June we began rehearsing for sessions on *Autoamerican*. Before going into the studio I went to England to do the "Muppet Show" and we had to decide who was going to produce the record.

After the success of "Call Me," we thought it would be great to work with Giorgio, but we had to consider our great success and relationship with Mike Chapman, and there were also the band's different opinions to take into account. Clem wanted to go to Sweden and work with Abba. Then he wanted to go to London and work with Paul McCartney at Abbey Road. We considered Phil Spector, too. And Chris was falling in love with Chic at the time. We were happy that "Call Me" had been a black crossover. We very consciously wanted to go against everything we'd done previously. Chris wanted to do things that were much different from the usual Blondie sound. Vocally I wanted to do something different, so I tried inhaling helium, which no one liked. Above all we wanted to stay home in New York to record.

However, our next stop was L.A., the city of lost angels, because the final group selection of Mike Chapman meant that we had to go out there. Mike had made the two previous records in New York, and he's under the most pressure, working the longest hours, so it was better for the whole project and meant we could work longer if he were allowed to bum out at home in his own element, instead of being forced to endure granite canyon national cemetery, Manhattan. I think it must be pretty obvious since we haven't been performing publicly that there was something amiss with Blondie as a touring band, but Blondie in the recording studio with Mike Chapman

Graffitti artist, Lee.

is a different thing. He is able to make the combination work.

Basic tracks are a long haul and we attempted to adjust to the slow studio routine. They took over a month. "Rapture" was recorded twice, once slower than the current release. The feel of the songs was closely examined. There were plenty of differences of opinion. Lots of time was spent discussing, hacking it out, trying to satisfy everyone. "Do The Dark" was written late one night on a cassette machine. "T-Birds" was named after the L.A. girls' roller derby team. The percussion on "Tide Is High" included eight tracks of drumsticks tapping on a piano bench. Chapman hunched over the console into the wee hours. People were pressed flat against the back wall of the studio by his playback volume. Gallons of José Cuervo Gold were consumed.

All that stood between the lounge of Studio A and one of the sleaziest pockets of Sunset Strip were two huge glass doors. As we sat watching TV and the Strip pass by, day turned into hot glowing night, the smog crept in, and winos, hookers, and assorted flotsam drifted by. They all seemed to stare in at us and we started to feel like babies behind glass. L.A.'s not really a tough town. It has a strange feeling of fragility. Earthquakes on the brain may be part of the reason why the surface always seems about to crack with delicate tension. New Yorkers start to snap

after about two weeks and soon the symptoms of California crazy began to appear.

Driving is a religion in L.A. and the air space around one's car (psychic territory) extends farther than anywhere else in the world. In other words, "Don't get too close to my car or your ass is grass." Cars in L.A. are extensions of one's body like nowhere else, so to get into the swing of things Blondie started eating cars and I mean *cars*. Long-suffering tour manager Bruce Patron spent his afternoons at Budget Rent-a-Bomb trading Chryslers for Trans Ams and back again. A white Lincoln Mark V convertible was the winner. Someone had dumped a gallon of Coca-Cola in the back seat, then parked it in the weeds for three days, and several million ants had invaded and occupied it. Their removal seemed impossible.

One of the best things about L.A. is Rodney Bingenheimer's radio show on KROQ in Pasadena. Over the years many of the greats have gone on, but Rodney still remains in the eye of the hurricane. One wall of his studio, covered by pictures of Rodney with almost every major rock star—Hendrix, Elvis, the Stones—says it all. His radio show started playing hard punk music, then power pop, followed by a brief foray into Shaun Cassidy, Bay City Rollers, glitter rock, then came full circle back to hard punk. Black Flag, The Circle Jerks, and the Surf Punks repre-

Tricia Gruen and Walter Steding.

sented the forefront of the new teenage bands while we were there.

As the sessions ground on, L.A. was into its worst smog alert in twelve years, and the populace began to enter the twilight zone. The smog crept under the windowsills and around corners; only the capsule-like air-conditioned vacuum of the studio was safe. Breathing smog is like eating angel dust burgers at the beach and getting sand in them that enters your brain and grits around. It's very abrasive, but good for the complexion.

Mike was called home to Australia on family business and we were adrift for a week, during which I honestly don't remember much of anything but something must have happened in the smog. Finally he returned, and sessions resumed slightly jet-lagged and hungover. The basic tracks wound down and we moved a block down the Strip to Studio B. The move marked the home stretch, the vocals, overdubs, and finally the orchestra, and horns.

Studio B is Mike Chapman's magic room. In days gone by these brown burlap walls saw the likes of the Righteous Brothers, Jan and Dean, Johnny Rivers, and The Beach Boys come and go. Now the control room is filled with a gigantic blue console that's hooked up to computers, satellites, and submarines off the coast of Maine. Here the songs get the chrome put on. Tom Scott added the final funk punch to

"Rapture." To unlock ourselves we employed outside musicians including a thirty-piece string section for Chris's "Europa" and a jazz combo to back me on "Faces." Mike also encouraged us to get away from standard rock. We didn't want to do what everybody expected us to do, which would have been "Call Me" type stuff. Ray Brown carefully worked out "Faces." Flo and Eddie went berserk and spread mayhem (they were off to Tuff Gong studios in Jamaica to record The Turtles' greatest hits in reggae). The orchestral session was tumultuous. Thirty of the greatest old players in Hollywood turned out for the session by maestro Jimmy Haskell. Some of these guys played with Tommy Dorsey, a couple even played on the sound track of Lawrence of Arabia! Things got more and more cataclysmic every day as the smog built up. We saw lights in the sky.

One day Orson Welles was in another room recording his voice for something (wildlife, wine), and Perry Como was recording his "Christmas in Israel" special with what sounded like the Mormon Tabernacle Choir, when some kid backed up about 200 feet into the parking lot across the way from the building and then floored it, driving smack into the wall of the studio making a big hole, a mess, and pretty much totaling what turned out to be his girlfriend's Audi. The kid's name was Jeffrey, his girlfriend's name was Suzy. They had a fight on the way to get blood tests

Mike Chapman.

The hands of Chapman.

Jean-Michel Basquait.

Snuky Taite and Fab Five Freddie Braithwaite.

for their marriage license, so Jeffrey got pissed and the rest is history on the B side of the "Tide Is High" single. That was the official excuse anyway—we wondered because Suzy and Jeffrey were in a black leather rock band called Deprogrammer and Jeff happened to have copies of his new single "Slammed In The Door" in the back seat of the former Audi. Luckily no one was hurt at all and the police were merciful and didn't drag Jeffrey off to the slammer. Anyway, that's what the song "Suzy and Jeffrey" is all about.

On *Autoamerican,* we wanted to expand. The whole thing about Blondie is its expansion. We got tired of the narrowness and limitations as to what we were allowed to do, and what we couldn't do, imposed by ·expectations based on our past performances. There are crazy restrictions at every level of the record business, like black people can't play a certain kind of music. You take a punk with a safety pin through his cheek and play him Haydn and he gets nervous and uptight. This is a purely intellectual reaction, not based on the music at all. It's only based on your preconceptions, and who you think listens to that music. I'm against this kind of musical narrowmindedness. If you do what you do and you don't take risks, people stop being excited about you. We buy music to create private moods, and atmosphere. We hear symphonies and theme music all the time. We know what Spanish and African music

sounds like. We're not locked into one form of music. With *Autoamerican* we tried to break away and make the album a surprise. There was a running joke in the studio that it was going to sell fourteen copies and get awards from critics, or critics were going to hate it and it would sell millions. I love it. We took a chance and did something different. Although *Autoamerican* is just an extension of what we've been doing since our first day, it's more obvious because we're better at it. "Rapture" is a combination of "Heart of Glass" and "Attack of the Giants Ants." We always held up David Bowie as an example for turning over his style. But what I see happening in the record industry seems to be happening in all related art forms. The overgrown monolithic corporations are going to be valued for what they are—quantity—and the small businesses and individual artists, who put more care into their work, will prevail. While we were making *Autoamerican, Union City* came out in New York and got good reviews, and I was pleased about that.

POST AUTOAMERICAN: NOVEMBER 1980- AUGUST 1981

By the time we'd finished *Autoamerican,* however, Blondie was not changing enough for my tastes. We

Debbie with her new hairdresser.

were worried that it was becoming a static safety thing that was there. Everyone could just step into it and there would be an audience and money. This has never been my goal. If Blondie ceased being a touring band after the last British tour, the split widened further when we took a break from being a recording band after *Autoamerican*. However, we still exist. Rock'nroll groups whose goal is to make money reach a point at which they die. On the way back down— and it is the way down—they just find that everything falls out from underneath them little by little, and they're stuck in this shell, this little ball out of which there's no way they can break and become plastic again. It's unfortunate that that's what happens, but that's just the nature of the business.

Everything comes down to how you put the jigsaw puzzle together. A lot of it has to do with what you arrange for yourself in terms of your commercial freedom. Basically what you have to do is define your art very carefully to yourself and commit yourself for a certain period of time to doing commercial interpretations of your art, making money and becoming financially independent so that you can be personally and artistically what you want to be. The choice is how much time you want to devote to struggling in the commercial world before closing off and doing what you want.

In the past artists have been the ones who've broken out, fought repression, and forced businessmen

to follow, but artists have fallen completely into the hands of businessmen everywhere. The problem comes when you start getting the art confused with the salesmanship.

By making music that was already in people's heads we had tried to tap into the universal unconscious. I think the best groups have always been the ones that work with the archetypes of music. The Beatles tapped into that. That's why the music's so appealing to everybody. It's the same as classical music.

The riddle of the existence of Blondie and our activities is involved with maintaining the illusion of success. What will they do to follow it up? Every time we do something we have to set precedents because we started by setting precedent, because then no one knows what to expect.

When we went out to L.A. to do *Solid Gold* at the beginning of 1981, the Iranians had been holding a bunch of Americans hostage in the American embassy in Tehran, and this had provided a morbid focus of attention for the American media. Whole TV news shows had been built around the unfortunate incident. The week the hostages were returned, we were driving through L.A. when a DJ came on the radio and started raving about "The Tide Is High" being the No. 1 song, the hostages being returned, and these events representing some kind of new dawning for America.

Debbie discussing the lyrics for Polyester with Bill Murray and his nephew.

John Waters, Debbie, Tab Hunter.

Debbie with Nile Rodgers.

Debbie with Bernard Edwards.

Debbie with the King.

We made the "Rapture" videotape, and continued to see more of Nile Rodgers and Bernard Edwards from Chic after they came on Glen O'Brien's show one night. Chris and I talked about asking them to produce my first solo album. Little by little we started getting more social and talked about doing a record together. We mentioned it to Nile and he said, "Yeah yeah yeah." But they must have talked about it too, because when I formally asked Nile one night, "Are you or aren't you? Shall we or shan't we?" he said we should. That's when we started really talking about what we wanted to do together musically.

Although Blondie and its image developed in one way and Chic and its image developed in another, both groups are musically broad, and I thought it would be interesting and exciting to work with Nile and Bernard. We have similar backgrounds and we still live a few blocks from each other. We planned to draw from both the producers' and artists' experiences. This was one of the few times that Nile and Bernard made the songwriting effort into a total collaboration with the artist. They usually reserve that area for themselves.

I thought the collaboration would be very successful. Then Nile took us out in his speedboat one early spring morning on the East River—which is full of floating telephone poles and other debris that can flip a boat over—and tried to kill us. The boat was going bam/bam/bap/bap on top of the water. We had to hold on for dear life. I liked it, but I was screaming and Tony Thompson was up front screaming too. Nile was driving us all crazy, because he likes to go so fast, and we were in terror throughout the ride. Suddenly we were at the beginning of the bay heading out toward Long Island. The swells were huge, there was a big wind, and we went right over a huge log. Nile said, "Oh I didn't even see that. Where did that come from?" That's when we realized the water was too high and everybody went berserk, cursing at Nile, who was having a great time, to slow down.

After he nauseated us on this boat ride, Nile decided to take us out to lunch, and even though we were thrashed to bits, we all went. That boat was so powerful it was like cruising down the river in a Sherman tank. Actually, I think it would have been calmer in a tank.

We didn't play with Nile and Bernard much before going into the studio. We knew what each other's stuff sounded like so we just went and did it. While we were recording they told a lot of race jokes and tried to make us feel inferior for being white, but it was just in fun. Their sense of humor is quite similar to Mike Chapman's, so perhaps we can conclude that the secret of being a good producer is being over-the-top crazy in the studio. Nile and Bernard definitely are. They're also very superior type of people; if you

Giger with the gold.

hang around with them they'll start putting you down anyway. It took five weeks to make *Koo Koo*.

We wanted to shift the image radically on this album. Ever since we'd met H. R. Giger at the Hansen Gallery in New York nearly two years earlier, similar loves for science fiction, skulls, and pagan archetypes had forged an automatic union, and we'd thought of working together. He had just come off a promotional tour of the *Alien* art, attended the Academy Awards, come to New York to do the gallery show, and was consequently fatigued and jet-lagged—something we had been through many times before as a hard touring band—so we felt sympathy with him from the start, and brought him over to our apartment. He implied he wanted to do a portrait of me and I was very flattered. Therefore, when we had to decide who was going to do the *Koo Koo* cover, a phone call was made, arrangements discussed, and Giger was immediately on the job. Working from a head shot by English photographer Brian Aris, he did four massive airbrushed paintings.

After we finished *Koo Koo* we made plans to go to Switzerland to work with Giger on two promotional videos for it. We felt we had really accomplished something in making a successful fusion of rock and R&B, which hadn't really been done on that level before, so we were very positive about the record, and equally excited about Giger's cover.

The week before we left Anya Phillips, who had been ill with cancer for two years, died. If Shoo Bee Doo's death marked the end of the glitter period, Anya's death seemed to mark something, perhaps the coming of the real world, as John Lennon's death certainly had months earlier in a larger sense. The period 1975–1980 was a time in which people insisted on being allowed to do what they weren't supposed to do. Anya symbolized that period. She was a powerful energy source that's now missing from the scene, an example of how intense willpower is charisma. As a Chinese woman she was a symbol of intensity, but she was also very romantic even though she would say hard things and act cold sometimes. I think Anya meant many things to everybody because she was so ferociously strong. Most of the people who started at the same level she did never got anywhere. Apart from being a photographer and actress, Anya succeeded in the things she tried. She helped shape the concept of the Contortions. I guess certain sections of a scene always get marked off by death. Anya's was a particularly personal loss for us. I wish she hadn't died.

The day we left for Europe it was boiling hot in the apartment after we had turned off the air conditioner in order to lock up. During that last half hour, we were dripping with sweat and the phone was ringing every five seconds. We have to change our number

171

T.V. Party.

every six months now because everybody finally gets it and instead of calling the office they all call here. Whatever, we finally left, arriving at the airport looking like we swam there.

When we landed in Zurich to do the taping, we didn't even know whether Giger, his wife Mia, and manager Ueli Steinly would be there. But they were, in their customary colors: Giger and wife in black and Steinly—to add the opposite—all in white. It set the stage for our visit. Giger lives in a couple of modest, simple houses he's combined to create a home and studio in a quiet section of Zurich. Outside was like the rest of the neighborhood—only his garden, running wild with untrimmed shrubbery (growth which he purposely allowed because he liked the random images and shapes that happened), suggested the atmosphere inside.

H. R. Giger is a man easily misunderstood. With his intense fascination for bones and skulls, he's been accused of black magic and witchcraft. To many, he seems like unleashed voodoo hell. In Switzerland he's known among journalists as Horror Rex. When the movie *Alien* came out it was Giger's designs that stirred up all the pseudo-sensationalist bullshit. He became internationally notorious, and the *Alien* images were banned. Giger even scared himself one night when he went to brush his teeth and ran into his alien model in the dark.

When *Koo Koo* came out there was the same intense reaction. "Did you hear about your cover being banned by British Rail?" asked an English journalist during a phone interview while we were in Switzerland. That was the first we heard of the reaction. Then the BBC banned the cover from TV because it was too disturbing.

Meanwhile, like the image of the Phantom of the Opera looming over his organ all hours of the night, Giger was completely immersed in his work on the two video productions. From the moment we arrived he had been firing questions at us to work out the concepts he had in mind. Shooting took four days. The last day was total panic. A Swiss-German friend of Giger's was shooting a documentary of us doing the video and a BBC film crew was shooting us shooting the video, while being filmed for the documentary. This was reminiscent of the 1979–80 New Year's Eve concert we did in Glasgow when 20/20 was shooting a documentary of us and the BBC was filming the concert. At first the BBC director said he could see how someone wouldn't want to have breakfast at Giger's every day, but finally we nearly had to throw him out he became so comfortable. However, I must say the best part of the English media is the BBC. They're professionals, they're openminded, and they do unusual programs. The fact that it's run by the government is also noteworthy. The BBC are

Glenn O'Brien and Walter Steding.

Rodney Bingenheimer.

Anya Phillips and James Chance.

174

The girls: Chrissie, Debbie, Viv, Poly, Siouxsie, Pauline.

Debbie with Muppets and Jim Henson.

Ambush!

Debbie with Eddie Murphy, Saturday Night Live.

simply extremely good at what they do and we always enjoyed working with them. During all this, we were making photographs of our own. If any scene had us swimming in opposites, and layers upon layers, just like Giger's work, it was this, our final one.

He exposed us to his world and we exposed Giger to a little of ours when we flew to England together after the taping. He seemed a little bemused and caught off guard by all the fans and star treatment, and we kidded him in our brash, curt but not disrespectful American way, but he soon got used to it.

When we got back from Europe we strapped on the gunbelts once more for some *Koo Koo* promo in New York. We also heard a professor at Harvard had the record removed from a campus record store because he freaked out when he saw the cover. He thought it was too gruesome or horrible.

●   ●   ●

The older I get the better I feel. I had the weight of the world on me when I was younger, and I was very unsure a lot of the time, out of touch, and half of what I should have been. Now that my other half is here too I'm very happy. I'm glad I'm doing what I'm doing. When I see myself doing something and I'm satisfied with it, it's the best feeling. That's what everybody wants.

When you're a kid you always see everything so simply and clearly because your life is so simple, but reportedly education keeps getting worse and worse. Every year, each generation of kids that goes through public school has a lousier and lousier education. I believe schizophrenia is one of the prime movers of our society. In our case schizophrenia makes me see that giving up and stopping is the same as keeping going. People give up too easily because they think it's a solution.

Work is important, but I don't think a person's goal in life is to work; it's to attain some higher spiritual state, to conquer our fears and paranoias, and ultimately to conquer fear of death and die consciously in peace. However, you cannot find peace until your surroundings are peaceful. I think the concept of the nuclear family is misleading, because people should owe allegiance to everybody. Nuclear families frustrate this goal by dividing people. The people in the streets are connected to the people in the apartments. We are all one thing, so at the moment we can only find a certain degree of peace.

If there is one root problem it's this duality we suffer from. Through man's foolishness everything gets divided into subject and object, the observer and the observed, and you cannot separate one from another. Our thoughts and words are as strong as our actions. When we see everything more the way it is, as displays of matter, formed by molecules and atoms, we won't be able to hurt each other so easily, because we will realize that every time we hurt someone else we're hurting ourselves.

THE GHOST OF SUNDAY MAN

As I've said, four years ago, while we were on tour, our cat Sunday Man ran away from my sister's house in the pouring rain while she was moving. Since then she has moved back to that house, which her husband had been renting to another family, and while walking to work earlier this week she said she thought she saw Sunday Man sitting on the front porch of one of the houses about half a mile farther down the block. We went down to the house where she saw the cat and spoke to the owner. She said it wasn't her cat—she had two dogs—but that the man next door had found a cat a few years back. She didn't want to commit herself further than to say that the man was crazy about the cat although he didn't like animals, which made me feel even more that this must be Sunday Man because he was a terrifically intelligent and sophisticated cat. Could it be that Sunday Man has survived?

NEW YORK

One night driving home from a party we passed CBGB's and stopped for a minute, remembering a hot summer night years ago when everybody was standing around with the winos out front. Legs McNeil and John Holmstrom were sharing a beer. Roberta was at the door hassling adroitly with hulking macho drunks. Arturo was prowling around in his mask. The guys from Television were standing against the wall looking neurotic. Richard Lloyd was sleeping in the shadows. Anya was packed into a cocktail dress carrying a cigarette holder. Terry Ork was scurrying around making deals. And, off in the deepest shadows, were row upon row of burned-out vestiges of glitter-queen rock stars with high platform heel boots, makeup, and really tight pants. Some fucked-up scabby winos were trying to grub cigarettes, matches, quarters, dimes, anything. Everyone was relaxed.

As far as the future is concerned, the Brattles represent the third to fifth generation rock'nroll band, depending on where you're counting from, at the beginning of the new era. The Brattles are Eric Emerson's children—Branch Emerson and Emerson Forth Emerson—and three other boys aged eight through twelve—Dagan Podlewsky, Jason Collins, and Vern Tetrikat. Elda Gentile, who used to work with us in the Stillettoes, is Branch's mother. Jane Forth, who was living with Eric when we first met him, is Emerson's mother. It's a neat, interesting, true connection,

and exciting because of what it represents. Kids this age are really starting to do something. They can really play, they have something to say, and it's funny. They're copying everything. They did a cover of "Houndog." Branch was dressed up like Paul Revere and the Raiders. They were all dressed totally differently, with a little glitter here and there.

Giger told us no city inspired him as much as New York. He thinks the subways and machines in the ground and the big office buildings growing up into the sky make it an enormous upside-down crucifix. He says New York is black magic. Out-of-towners always talk about its fast tempo, but this racing pulse of New York is an illusion. The tempo is not any faster than anywhere else. It might even be a little bit slower. The many layers of activity in a relatively small space add to the confusion. Acting under this illusion of speed you can probably move too fast in New York and consequently miss connections. When I first came here in 1965, I was moving too fast but, thinking that I was missing everything, tried to go faster, when actually I should have just slowed down.

On an average day I get up around noon. Sometimes we go out and run around to business offices, magazine offices, or to management, trying to keep everything going, until the late afternoon. I get home around six P.M. and watch the news, which is always entertaining, then the wrestling. Sometimes Chris and I get so excited by the TV match we start wrestling with each other. On the other hand, we often stay in all day doing business over the phone and entertaining guests. Chris is always saying how much he hates to go out, but we go out three or four times a week without realizing it. There's so many exciting possibilities and invitations in Manhattan, before you know it you go through three or four and then that's enough. Sometimes none is enough. Other times the days and nights aren't long enough.

I do think we should try to upgrade our values, because everything in the world is getting so fucked up with the depletion of natural resources, time is getting short. We have to come to grips with it. In the seventies it wasn't hip to be good it was hip to be hip, chic, smooth, witty, or fast. The rules of the game generally are if you can screw somebody and get away with not paying for something, make somebody else pay the price. We saw ample proof of corruption, exposés, etc. At the moment people are less concerned with being good and apparently more concerned with their own survival. The very styles that we created in the sixties and mid-seventies are now being sent back against us in mass-produced death. People are being strangled by misinterpretations, killed, destroyed, spat on, and disgustingly treated. The murder of John Lennon brought it all home. Many of our heroes have been shot.

If the proper ritual is followed, it has some kind of electromagnetic implication so that, further on down the line, more and more of your circuits will be completed. You'll consequently be able to do what you want, which is what magic is. Summoning up our own magic on a daily basis is what we always strive to do. I think everyone gets high because there's no more magic. Especially younger kids. Getting high is

Graffitti.

Burns guitars.

Please do not walk on the wings while the plane is in motion.

Airport life.

The Moon.

Mona.

an expression for the magic we are taught doesn't exist. If we were taught that magic exists, we'd be looking for our own magic inside ourselves and getting a little peace of mind, but organized western religion has taught us that what's inside us is evil, sin, and violence, so we learned not to seek inside ourselves but to stay outside all the time.

Sometimes I come home after a day feeling spent and I look at the different things that happened to me during the day, and all of them were great and I go, "What the fuck?" I'm incredibly oversensitive thinking about what this person said, or what that one meant. When I'm lying in bed I get flashbacks of every little word, every little sentence, every little movement of an intricate day, and I can't sleep. It keeps going like a movie. On the other hand, I think that you're better off when you see things differently than other people. That's what makes you you.

The Orchestra.

Interior Giger's studio, Zurich.

Giger as the magician.

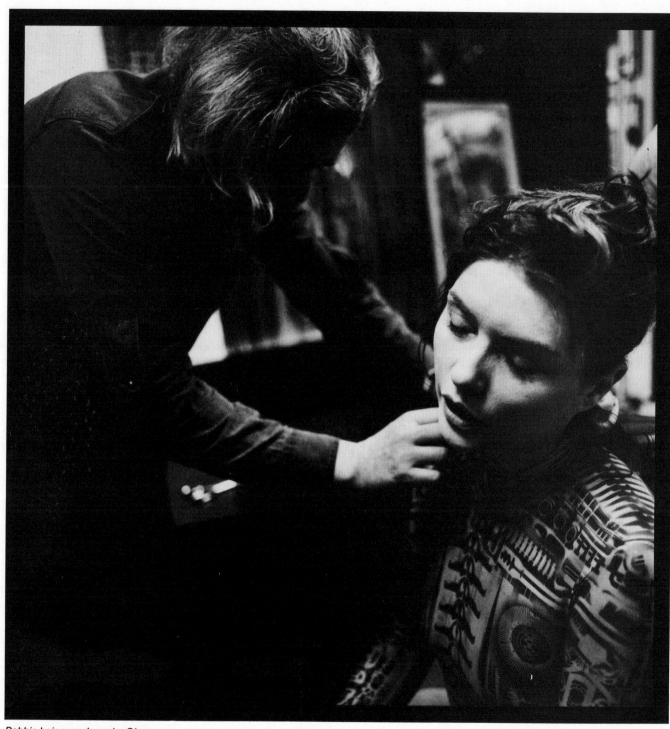

Debbie being made up by Giger.

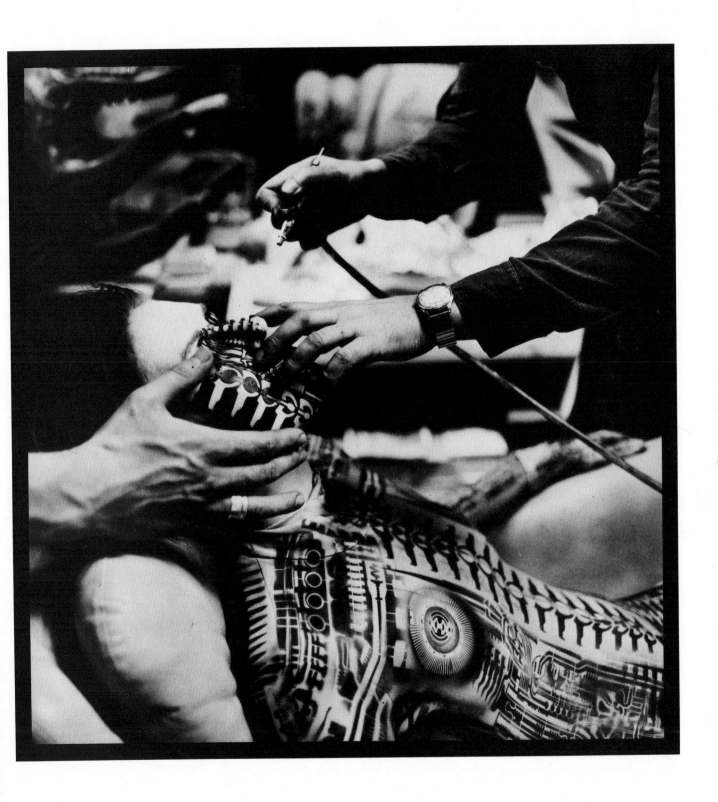

Now I Know You Know *promotional video, directed and with art work by Giger.*